ESSENTIAL ELEMENTS®
for *Strings*

TEACHER RESOURCE KIT
LESSON PLANS AND STUDENT ACTIVITY WORKSHEETS

HAL•LEONARD®
7777 W. BLUEMOUND RD. P.O. BOX 13819 MILWAUKEE, WI 53213

MW01055958

Authors of Essential Elements for Strings:

Michael Allen

Robert Gillespie

Pamela Tellejohn Hayes

Printed in the United States of America

Send all inquiries to:
Hal Leonard Corporation
7777 West Bluemound Road
Milwaukee, WI 53213

7777 W. BLUEMOUND RD. P.O. BOX 13819 MILWAUKEE, WI 53213

TABLE OF CONTENTS

TABLE OF CONTENTS

TO THE DIRECTOR

Welcome to the *Essential Elements for Strings* series. You have selected an outstanding method to introduce your students to the joys of making music and playing in the orchestra. As you review the contents of this *Teacher Resource Kit,* it is important to remember a few Essential Elements of successful teaching.

1. Make students feel welcome in your class. Learn each student's name.

2. Clearly define your class expectations by communicating:
   • how to enter the room.
   • where to put instrument cases.
   • when to unpack instruments.
   • what materials are needed for each class. (pencil, notebook, etc.)

3. Define your objective(s) for each daily lesson.

4. Assess student progress and achievement throughout, and at the end of the lesson.

5. Identify material for student review in preparation for the next class by:
   • using homework to reinforce concepts and material presented in class.
   • explaining practice tips to allow students to work alone effectively.

6. Share class expectations and communicate often with parents, classroom teachers and administrators through the use of:
   • personal notes to acknowledge effort.
   • personal phone calls to recognize student achievement.
   • a yearly calendar to publicize important dates early.

7. Intervene early when signs of frustration set in. Failure to complete assignments or discipline problems in class is often the result of the student's difficulty in mastering class material. You may wish to check:
   • the student's instrument, to see if it is working properly.
   • the student's comprehension of class material, i.e. note names, correct fingering.
   • physical elements such as posture and hand position.
   • other related problems that could be discussed with the school health aide, classroom teacher, or administrator.

Alert parents to these signs of frustration as soon as possible and keep a record of your communication with them.

8. Praise student effort and achievement often. Remember, "Praise Pays!"

9. Correct students in private. When doing so, make sure the student knows what behavior was unacceptable, why the behavior was unacceptable, and what the student needs to do to be a successful class (orchestra) member. Always focus on the behavior and not the person.

10. Consult **Essential Elements Orchestra Director's Communication Kit** for additional ideas and information.

USING THIS KIT

LESSON PLANS

Lesson plans provide an organized and consistent approach to instruction. *The lessons presented here do not necessarily correspond to one class period.* It may take one, two or several class periods to cover the materials presented in a single lesson. Grade level, compositional make-up of the group, size, class length and frequency of instruction will impact how much time is spent on each lesson. Remember, an effective teacher balances quantity with quality. A teacher should not feel pressured to complete Book 1 in a single year.

Activity

THEORY

Student activity worksheets have been developed to provide support materials to enhance learning and help develop comprehensive musicianship.

Some activities can be done in class while others may be used as homework assignments. Teachers should review each student's work and provide positive educational feedback. Keeping a portfolio of each student's work is one way to assess student progress and share accomplishments with parents, classroom teachers, general music teachers, and administrators.

Assessment

ASSESSMENT

Assessment sheets have been designed for every quiz. These have been coordinated with the name and number of each quiz that appears in the student book. A list of criteria is identified with a suggested number of points for each item. They may be used as printed, or as a guide for designing your own. There is additional assessment material related to performances and concert etiquette included at the end of this section.

HISTORY

The history of music from the Middle Ages through the Twentieth Century is included. Each page gives a brief summary of the musical developments during that particular era. Also included are important developments in art and literature, as well as a list of significant world events. Worksheets which could also be used as quizzes and an answer key are provided at the end of the section.

CD-ROM INSTRUCTIONS:

This CD-ROM contains "text-only" versions of the Lesson Plans and is designed to work with any word processing program. Copy these documents onto your desktop or word processing program to edit, personalize and print. Some documents, including worksheets/quizzes, are in PDF format and may be viewed and printed, but not altered. You will need Adobe® Acrobat® Reader® 4.0 to open these files. The installer is included on this CD-ROM.

CD-Rom

Reproducibles

The Listening Lessons found on this CD-ROM can be played on a CD player or a computer enabled for CD audio playback.

Listening

The minimum requirements needed to run this CD-ROM are as follows:

Minimum PC Requirements:	**Minimum Macintosh Requirements:**
Windows 95 B	PowerPC or higher
200 MHz processor	32 MB RAM
32 MB RAM	System 7.5.1
4X CD-ROM drive	4X CD-ROM drive

PLAY-ALONG CD DISC 1

A play-along CD that covers the first 71 exercises is included in every student book. From the very beginning, students can model tone production and technique by listening to a professional orchestra. The exercises are played twice – once with a full orchestra, and then again with accompaniment track only.

The accompaniment tracks are performed on real instruments and may be used to teach phrasing and dynamics, to encourage musicality, and to present music from a variety of styles and cultures.

NOTE: There are additional 2-CD paks to be used with Exercises 72 to the end of the book. These are available from your music dealer. As an alternative, MP3 files are available, without charge at http://www.halleonard.com. On the band/orchestra/jazz page click on the Essential Elements link and then click on the string link.

NATIONAL STANDARDS FOR ARTS EDUCATION
PERFORMING GROUPS Grades 5-8

The *National Standards for Arts Education* were developed by the Consortium of National Arts Education Associations under the guidance of the National Committee for Standards in the Arts. The Standards were prepared under a grant from the U.S. Department of Education, the National Endowment for the Arts, and the National Endowment for the Humanities.

This series, *Essential Elements for Strings,* is based on the National Standards. By structuring this course of study around the National Standards, teachers and their students may begin to construct a vital relationship with the arts, and in so doing, as with any subject, approach this curriculum with discipline and study. The National Standards spell out what every young musician should know about the arts and provide a framework for achieving these goals.

Outlined below, you will find a complete listing of the *National Standards for Arts Education* – Music, including both the Content Standards (listed in **BOLD** typeface) and the Achievement Standards (listed in standard typeface). In this *Teacher Resource Kit,* each specific Learning Objective is identified with the corresponding National Standard, i.e. *The student will read, count and perform dotted half notes.* (**National Standard** 5)

1. SINGING, ALONE AND WITH OTHERS, A VARIED REPERTOIRE OF MUSIC

The focus of this series, *Essential Elements for Strings,* is the study of music through instrumental performance. While we believe that singing is important to all music study, our emphasis here must be on instrumental skill development. Students should be encouraged to sing throughout their study of music and teachers may wish to incorporate this standard in the following ways:

• singing rhythm studies as well as clapping or tapping them.

• singing pitches while practicing fingerings.

• singing musical examples or exercises to help develop the idea of phrase shape and intonation.

• other creative ideas as supplied by the individual teacher.

2. PERFORMING ON INSTRUMENTS, ALONE AND WITH OTHERS, A VARIED REPERTOIRE OF MUSIC

A. Students perform on at least one instrument accurately and independently, alone and in small and large ensembles, with good posture, good playing position, and good breath, bow, or stick control.

B. Students perform with expression and technical accuracy on at least one string, wind, percussion, or classroom instrument a repertoire of instrumental literature with a level of difficulty of 2, on a scale of 1 to 6.

C. Students perform music representing diverse genres and cultures, with expression appropriate for the work being performed.

D. Students play by ear simple melodies on a melodic instrument and simple accompaniments on a harmonic instrument.

E. Students perform with expression and technical accuracy a varied repertoire of instrumental literature with a level of difficulty of 3, on a scale of 1 to 6, including some solos performed from memory.

HOW TO USE ESSENTIAL ELEMENTS LESSON PLANS

WHY USE LESSON PLANS

Lesson plans help a teacher efficiently instruct and organize long- and short-term goals for their students. The purpose of the lesson plans in the *Teacher Resource Kit* is to provide teachers with guidelines for instructing their students through step-by-step mastery of each skill and concept. No two classes learn in exactly the same way and at exactly the same rate. *Essential Elements* lesson plans are designed as a resource to help teachers save time in best determining the unique needs of their individual teaching situations.

HOW THE LESSON PLANS ARE ORGANIZED...

Essential Elements lesson plans are divided into six sections:

- OBJECTIVES
- WARM-UP/REVIEW
- STRATEGIES FOR TEACHING OBJECTIVES
- MOTIVATION
- ASSESSMENT OF OBJECTIVES
- CLOSURE

1. Objectives

Instructional OBJECTIVES are stated at the beginning of each lesson plan. These reflect the concepts and skills that students should be able to demonstrate at the end of the lesson. At the top of each lesson plan are the student book page number(s), Teacher's Manual page numbers and exercises that are included in the lesson plan.

2. Warm-Up/Review

Most successful classes start with a review of previously introduced concepts and playing skills. The purpose of WARM-UP/REVIEW activities is to enable the teacher to reinforce skills and concepts so that students may securely master them. Teachers should use any previously described strategies for teaching the review activities, or ones that they design themselves.

3. Strategies For Teaching Objectives

The STRATEGIES FOR TEACHING OBJECTIVES are designed to suggest methods of helping students learn to achieve the instructional objectives listed at the beginning of a lesson plan. For convenience, the numbers of the suggested strategies are directly correlated to the numbers of the lesson plan objectives, i.e., strategy "1" corresponds to objective "1."

NOTE: Multiple strategies for the same objective are labeled "1a., 1b., 1c.," etc.

4. Motivation

Activities designed to motivate students are an important part of a successful string class. These often fun, challenging activities foster students' enthusiasm for playing and develop their commitment to practicing and playing stringed instruments. One suggested MOTIVATION activity is included in each lesson plan.

5. Assessment Of Objectives

An integral part of string class teaching is the assessment of student learning. Only when a teacher knows what students have learned can he/she effectively plan instruction for future classes. The ASSESSMENT OF OBJECTIVES describes activities designed to assess student achievement of the instructional objectives listed at the beginning of each Essential Elements lesson plan. The numbering of the assessment activities is correlated to the numbering of each lesson plan, i.e., assessment activity number "1" is designed to help assess student achievement of objective "1."

6. Closure

Activities that end a class period help summarize what has been presented and give students direction for reinforcing what has been introduced. CLOSURE activities include summarizing the concepts and skills presented, reminding students how to practice to continue learning what has been presented and making assignments for the next class based upon student performance.

USING LESSON PLANS SUCCESSFULLY

Lesson plans are essential to effective string teaching. However, a key element in successful teaching is how the teacher presents the lesson plan to students. The results of research and critical observation of successful teaching reveal many factors in addition to well-designed lesson plans that contribute to effective teaching:

These factors include:

- The teacher constantly moving throughout the classroom checking student posture, instrument position, left hand skills, bowing, etc.

- The teacher physically assisting students in achieving correct playing posture and technique.

- The teacher modeling and demonstrating the playing skills students are learning.

- The teacher maintaining a very high standard of tone quality and intonation.

- The teacher relating to students in a way that is appropriate for the age and learning styles of the students.

- The teacher *carefully* developing students' playing skills, allowing students to master one skill before attempting to learn a new skill.

Keep all of these factors in mind when using the *Teacher Resource Kit* to plan your teaching.

LESSON PLANS

The following lesson plans are also provided on the enclosed CD-ROM. Edit, adapt, and personalize the documents to meet the needs of your program. In addition, the original purchaser of this book is granted permission to duplicate these pages. They may be reduced, enlarged, or adapted for any non-profit use.

UNIT 1 LESSON ONE

OBJECTIVES	NATIONAL STANDARDS
At the end of instruction students should be able to:	
1. Demonstrate how to unpack and pack their instruments.	
2. Identify one element of individual instrument history.	9
3. Identify parts of the instrument.	2
4. Describe proper care of the instrument.	2
5. Demonstrate proper instrument position.	2
6. Identify and pizzicato each open string.	2

STRATEGIES FOR TEACHING OBJECTIVES

1a. Ask students to place instruments on the left side of their chair. Violin/viola cases should be flat on the floor with the handle facing them. Cellos/basses should rest on their side.

1b. Show violin/viola students how to open their cases, then ask them to imitate.

1c. Ask cello/bass students to remove their bows from their cases and place the bows in a safe place. Remind them always to remove the bow from the case first and replace it last. Show them how to remove the instrument from the case and ask them to imitate.

2. Ask students to read individual instrument histories while their instruments are being tuned.

3a. Point to the parts of the instrument and have students find them on their own instrument.

3b. Ask students to study the picture on pg. 2 (TM pgs. 35–36).

4a. Ask students to take turns reading aloud the Take Special Care section on pg. 2 (TM pgs. 35–36).

4b. Give students additional instructions on caring for their instrument (TM pg. 259).

5. Demonstrate your preferred method of holding each instrument (TM pgs. 37–38). Note: The authors have experienced the greatest success in their own classrooms by starting violin/viola students in "guitar" position first until their left hand shape has been properly established, usually about the time the D Major scale has been learned. This allows students the opportunity to see their left hand shape more accurately and prevents the tension that can be created by trying to support the instrument on the shoulder before the proper psychomotor development has occurred.

6a. Teach students the names of the open strings.

6b. Play the pitches of the open strings and ask students to pizzicato them on their instrument.

6c. Ask each section to pizzicato their open strings from highest to lowest.

6d. Play various patterns, using open strings, i.e., DDDD, AAAA, DDAA and AADD and ask students to echo.

MOTIVATION

Select one student to pizzicato a four-note pattern and let the remainder of the class echo.

ASSESSMENT OF OBJECTIVES

1. Observe students packing and/or unpacking their instruments.

2. Ask students to identify a famous maker of their instrument.

3. Point to various parts of the instrument and ask students to identify them.

4. Ask students to list the important elements of caring for their instrument.

5. Observe the instrument position of each student.

6. Have individual sections pizzicato open strings four times each, from highest to lowest, and say the name of the string out loud as they play.

CLOSURE

- Remind students to care for their instruments properly.

- Remind students not to play with the bow until instructed to do so.

- Remind students of correct position/posture while practicing.

- Assign practice material based upon class performance.

UNIT 1 LESSON TWO

OBJECTIVES	NATIONAL STANDARDS
At the end of instruction students should be able to:	
1. Define beat, music staff, bar line and measure.	5
2. Define quarter note and quarter rest.	5
3. Define pizzicato.	5
4. Pizzicato open D and A strings while following a line of music.	2

WARM-UP/REVIEW

• Care of instrument

• Parts of instrument

• Names of open strings

• Proper playing position

STRATEGIES FOR TEACHING OBJECTIVES

1. Explain beat, music staff, bar lines and measures (TM pg. 39). Ask students to identify each element in their books.

2. Explain quarter note and quarter rest (TM pg. 39). Ask students to find examples of these in their books.

3. Define and demonstrate pizzicato.

4a. Using #2, *Let's Play Open "D,"* #3, *Let's Play Open "A,"* #4, *Two's A Team,* and #5, *At Pierrot's Door,* ask students to say or sing the letter names of the notes, saying the word "rest" on each quarter rest.

4b. Ask students to pizzicato #2–5 while continuing to say or sing the note names. Students should master each exercise before proceeding to the next one.

MOTIVATION

Teacher plays *At Pierrot's Door* with one wrong note and asks the students to raise their hands when they hear that note.

ASSESSMENT OF OBJECTIVES

1. Ask students to define beat, music staff, bar line and measure.

2. Ask students to draw quarter notes and quarter rests on the board.

3. Ask students to define pizzicato.

4. Ask students to perform #5, *At Pierrot's Door,* saying the names of the notes as they play.

CLOSURE

• Summarize new concepts.

• Remind students not to play with the bow until instructed to do so.

• Remind students of correct position/posture while practicing.

• Assign practice material based upon class performance.

UNIT 1 LESSON THREE

OBJECTIVES	NATIONAL STANDARDS
At the end of instruction students should be able to:	
1. Identify the clef sign for their own instrument.	5
2. Identify the names of the lines and spaces for their clef.	5
3. Define and identify time signature, double bar and repeat sign.	5
4. Demonstrate counting and tapping toes while playing open D and A strings pizzicato.	5

WARM-UP/REVIEW

• Proper playing position

• Beat, music staff, bar lines and measure

• Quarter notes and quarter rests

• Location of D and A strings

STRATEGIES FOR TEACHING OBJECTIVES

1. Draw the clef sign for each instrument on the board.

2a. Draw a series of random notes on the board, some with lines through the note head and some without. Ask students to identify the difference between line notes and space notes.

2b. Ask students to hold one hand in front of them and turn it sideways. Relate the five fingers to the five lines of the music staff and the four spaces between the fingers to the four spaces on the music staff.

2c. Relate the names of the alphabet to the sequence of lines and spaces on a music staff.

2d. Ask students to look at the music staff at the top of the page and study the names of the lines and spaces.

3a. Allow individual students to read the definitions of time signature, double bar and repeat sign out loud.

3b. Ask students to find examples of these symbols somewhere else on the page.

4a. Ask students to tap their toe with a steady beat.

4b. Ask students to count out loud while continuing to tap their toe.

4c. Ask students to say/sing note names in #6, *Jumping Jacks,* while tapping toe with a steady beat.

4d. Ask students to say/sing note names in #7, *Mix 'em Up,* #8, *Count Carefully,* and #9, *Essential Elements Quiz* while plucking the correct string. Students should master each exercise before proceeding to the next one.

MOTIVATION

Ask one student to select one or more students to play one of the tunes from this lesson with him/her.

ASSESSMENT OF OBJECTIVES

1. Ask students to name their clef sign.

2. Draw notes on the music staff in different clefs and ask students to identify names of notes for their clef.

3. Ask students to define time signature, double bar and repeat sign.

4. Ask students to play #9, *Essential Elements Quiz,* while tapping their toe with a steady beat. A sample playing quiz is available on pg. 121 based on the objectives identified on TM pg. 45.

CLOSURE

- Summarize new concepts.

- Remind students not to play with the bow until instructed to do so.

- Remind students of correct position/posture while practicing.

- Assign practice material based upon class performance.

UNIT 1 LESSON FOUR

OBJECTIVES   NATIONAL STANDARDS

At the end of instruction students should be able to:

1. Shape left hand properly.	2
2. Define sharp.	5
3. Place G and F♯ on the fingerboard with the correct number of fingers.	2
4. Keep fingers down on one string, while plucking an open string (bass).	2
5. Pizzicato G and F♯ by ear.	2
6. Pizzicato G and F♯ while reading a printed line.	2

WARM-UP/REVIEW

• Music staff and note names

• Time signature, double bar and repeat sign

• Counting and tapping

• Quarter notes and quarter rests

STRATEGIES FOR TEACHING OBJECTIVES

1a. Ask students to study the picture of the shape for their left hand (TM pgs. 46–47).

1b. Explain the numbering system for each finger. (Note: Clarify for those who play piano that fingers are numbered differently on stringed instruments.) Ask them to imitate the picture in the book.

1c. Ask one instrument section at a time to bring their hand to the fingerboard and place it on the instrument.

1d. Move around the room as quickly as possible to individually assist students in developing proper left hand shape.

2. Read the definition of a sharp to the class.

3a. Explain to students which notes are played with which finger.

3b. Ask students to place their left hand on the instrument, then practice lifting different fingers on and off the string.

3c. Call out different note names – G and F♯ and ask students to put down the correct number of fingers on the string, without making any sound with the right hand. Do this several times until students feel comfortable lifting and setting fingers.

4. Demonstrate for the basses how to keep fingers down on the D string, while playing the open G string.

5a. Ask students to pizzicato the notes G and F♯ four times each.

5b. Play a series of notes and ask the students to echo them (TM pg. 48 – notice these examples include the E which is introduced on p. 7).

6. Pizzicato #10, *Let's Read "G,"* #11, *Let's Read "F♯,"* and #12, *Lift Off* while saying/singing note names. Encourage students to start memorizing the names of the notes. Students should master each exercise before proceeding to the next one.

MOTIVATION

Invite students to play the exercises in this lesson with the CD. Encourage them to play with the CD at home as well.

ASSESSMENT OF OBJECTIVES

1. Have students place their fingers on the note G (F♯ for basses). Instruct them to observe the check mark at the bottom of the page and compare their left hand position to the diagram at the top of the page. Move around the room as quickly as possible to verbally evaluate the students' left hand shapes using the following check points: fingers curved over strings, relaxed wrist, thumb shape and position. For violins and violas, it is very important that you also check for a square first finger shape.

2. Ask students to define sharp and point to a sharp sign in their books.

3. Call out a note name and ask students to place the correct number of fingers on the string.

4. Observe bass section during #12 to see if they are keeping their fingers down properly.

5. Ask individual students to echo four-note patterns.

6. Ask students to pizzicato #12 while saying/singing letter names of the notes. Ask one group to perform, while another group points to the notes in their books.

CLOSURE

- Summarize new concepts.

- Remind students not to play with the bow until instructed to do so.

- Remind students of correct position/posture while practicing.

- Assign practice material based upon class performance.

UNIT 2 LESSON ONE

OBJECTIVES	NATIONAL STANDARDS
At the end of instruction students should be able to:	
1. Shape right hand properly on a pencil, BOW BUILDER ONE.	2
2. Place E on the fingerboard with the correct number of fingers.	2
3. Pizzicato G, F♯, E and D while reading a printed line.	2
4. Draw a clef sign, time signature, and double bar.	5

WARM-UP/REVIEW

• Music staff and note names

• Left hand shape

• G and F♯

STRATEGIES FOR TEACHING OBJECTIVES

1a. Ask students to study the picture of the pencil hold.

1b. Explain and model steps 1–5. Work with violin/viola at the same time, then cello, then bass.

1c. Ask students to perform each step in BOW BUILDER ONE. Then move throughout the class as quickly as possible and give students manual assistance as needed.

2a. Ask students to shape left hand properly on the instrument and pizzicato #13, *On The Trail.*

2b. Ask students to lift fingers so only one finger is remaining on the string.

2c. Ask students to pizzicato that note.

2d. Ask students to locate E in #14, *Let's Read "E."*

2e. Ask students to play #14, *Let's Read "E"* while reading the printed music.

3a. Ask students to pizzicato the notes G, F♯, E and D, four times each.

3b. Play a series of notes and ask the students to echo play them (TM pg. 48).

3c. Pizzicato #15, *Walking Song,* and #16, *Essential Elements Quiz* while saying/singing note names. Students should master each exercise before proceeding to the next one.

4a. Ask students to draw the clef sign for their instrument on a piece of manuscript paper.

4b. Review the definition and placement of time signatures and double bar lines.

MOTIVATION

Invite students to create their own melodies for other students to echo.

ASSESSMENT OF OBJECTIVES

1. Ask students to place their fingers on a pencil as in BOW BUILDER ONE. Visually observe each student and reward them by giving them one point if the thumb is placed correctly and one point for each finger that is placed correctly (5 points total).

2. Ask all students to pizzicato the note E and visually observe their finger placement.

3. Ask students to pizzicato #15 while saying/singing letter names of notes. Ask small groups to perform, while others point to the notes in their books. Visually assess each group to see they are following the printed music correctly.

4. Ask students to complete #16, *Essential Elements Quiz*. Evaluate each student's work to see that the symbols have been drawn in the correct location.

5. Ask students to play #16, *Essential Elements Quiz*. A sample playing quiz is available on pg. 122 based on the objectives identified on TM pg. 55.

CLOSURE

- Summarize new concepts.

- Remind students not to play with the bow until instructed to do so.

- Remind students of correct position/posture while practicing.

- Assign practice material based upon class performance.

UNIT 2 LESSON TWO

OBJECTIVES	NATIONAL STANDARDS
At the end of instruction students should be able to:	
1. Perform pencil hold exercises, BOW BUILDER TWO.	2
2. Demonstrate bowing motions, BOW BUILDER THREE.	2
3. Name one characteristic of a folk song.	9
4. Pizzicato G, F♯, E and D with increased proficiency while reading a printed line of music.	2

WARM-UP/REVIEW

- Pencil hold

- *Listening Skills* (TM pg. 48)

- Counting and tapping

- Music staff and note names

STRATEGIES FOR TEACHING OBJECTIVES

1a. Ask students to shape their right hand properly on a pencil.

1b. Demonstrate each pencil hold exercise, then ask students to imitate. Remember to point out the differences in the bow hold for each instrument. Notice that the bass exercises are for the French bow only.

2a. Demonstrate BOW BUILDER THREE, *Swingin' Out* for violins/violas, *Elbow Energy* for cellos and *The Pendulum* for basses.

2b. Ask each instrument section to demonstrate their bowing motions for the class.

3. Ask one student to read the history of folk songs aloud to the class.

4. Pizzicato # 17, *Hopscotch*, #18, *Morning Dance*, and #19, *Rolling Along* while tapping toes and saying/singing letter names of the notes. Students should master each exercise before proceeding to the next one.

MOTIVATION

Challenge each instrument section to determine which section has the best bow hand shape.

ASSESSMENT OF OBJECTIVES

1. Ask students to perform each pencil hold exercise and visually assess their right hand shape.

2. Ask each instrument section to perform the appropriate bowing motion and visually assess their accuracy.

3. Ask students to name one characteristic of a folk song.

4. Divide students into small groups to play #19. While one group is playing pizzicato, all others should say/sing notes and tap toes. Check as each group plays to see that they are reading from the book and putting the correct finger(s) down for the corresponding notes.

CLOSURE

• Summarize new concepts.

• Remind students not to play with the bow until instructed to do so.

• Remind students of correct position/posture while practicing.

• Remind students of proper left and right hand shape.

• Assign practice material based upon class performance.

UNIT 2 LESSON THREE

OBJECTIVES	NATIONAL STANDARDS
At the end of instruction students should be able to:	
1. Place the instrument in shoulder position for violin/viola.	2
2. Demonstrate left hand Workouts.	2
3. Pizzicato the A on the G string for bass.	2
4. Keep fingers down on the D string while playing open A for violin, viola, and cello.	2
5. Pizzicato D, E, F♯, G and A while reading a printed line of music.	2, 5

WARM-UP/REVIEW

• Left hand shape

• BOW BUILDERS ONE, TWO AND THREE

• Counting and tapping

• Reading D, E, F♯ and G on a printed line of music

STRATEGIES FOR TEACHING OBJECTIVES

1. Ask violin/viola students to hold their instruments in shoulder position following steps 1–4 on p. 3 (TM pg. 37).

2a. Ask students to look at descriptions of left hand exercises in their book. Notice that bass players do not have these in their books; due to the fact that the space was needed to show both the German and French bow hand shapes. Basses should do the exercises shown for cellos.

2b. Demonstrate each of the exercises and have students follow by rote.

3. Explain the placement of first finger to produce the pitch A on the G string for the basses.

4a. Explain the purpose of the bracket in #20, *Good King Wenceslas* for violin, viola and cello.

4b. Ask violin, viola and cello students to put their fingers down on the note G on the D string, then pizzicato the A string without lifting any fingers.

5. Pizzicato #21, *Seminole Chant,* and #22, *Essential Elements Quiz – Lightly Row* while tapping their toe and saying/singing letter names of the notes. Students should master each exercise before proceeding to the next one.

MOTIVATION

Challenge each instrument section to determine which section has the best bow hand shape on a pencil.

ASSESSMENT OF OBJECTIVES

1. Violin/viola students hold their instruments in shoulder positioning. The teacher visually evaluates the placement of the instrument and gives each student verbal feedback. Ask violin/viola students to perform left hand exercises while cello/bass students observe, then switch sections.

2. Ask students to choose one Workout to demonstrate. Visually assess each student to see if they are using the correct motion.

3. While playing #20, *Good King Wenceslas,* observe the basses to see that students are placing first finger properly on the G string.

4. While playing #20, observe the violins, violas and cellos to see that they are keeping their fingers down where the brackets occur.

5. Ask students to play #22, *Essential Elements Quiz – Lightly Row* in small groups. While one group is playing pizzicato, all others should say/sing notes and tap toes. Check as each group plays to see that they are reading from the book and putting the correct finger(s) down for the corresponding notes. A sample playing quiz is available on pg. 123 based on the objectives identified on TM pg. 62.

CLOSURE

- Summarize new concepts.

- Remind students to do pencil exercises but not to get the bow out.

- Remind students not to play with the bow until instructed to do so.

- Remind students of correct position/posture while practicing.

- Remind students of proper left hand shape.

- Assign practice material based upon class performance.

UNIT 2 LESSON FOUR

OBJECTIVES	NATIONAL STANDARDS
At the end of instruction students should be able to:	
1. Locate third position (bass).	2
2. Identify note names on ledger lines for viola, cello and bass.	5
3. Place D and C♯ on the fingerboard with the correct fingers.	2
4. Pizzicato D and C♯ by ear.	2
5. Pizzicato D and C♯ while reading a printed line of music.	2

WARM-UP/REVIEW

• BOW BUILDERS ONE, TWO AND THREE

• Shoulder position for violin/viola

• Left hand *Workouts*

STRATEGIES FOR TEACHING OBJECTIVES

1a. Identify the location of third position for the basses.

1b. Ask basses to place their hands in third position and pizzicato the note D.

1c. Have basses check the new note to see if it blends with the open D string.

2a. Draw ledger lines on the board and place notes on them.

2b. Relate the lines and spaces of ledger lines to the alphabet.

3a. Ask students to place their fingers on the A string, G string for bass.

3b. Check for proper left hand shape.

3c. Ask students to look at the diagram at the top of pg. 10.

3d. Explain to students which notes are played with which finger.

3e. Let students practice lifting different fingers on and off the string.

3f. Call out D and C♯ and ask students to put down the correct number of fingers on the string without making any sound with the right hand. Do this several times until students feel comfortable lifting and setting fingers. Explain to students they can now play two Ds on their instrument - open D and "high" D.

4a. Ask students to pizzicato D and C♯, four times each.

4b. Play Listening Skills lines 1–3 (TM pg. 65) and ask students to echo them.

5. Students pizzicato #23, *Let's Read "D,"* #24, *Let's Read "C♯,"* #25, *Take Off,* #26, *Caribbean Island,* and #27, *Olympic High Jump* while saying/singing note names. Students should master each exercise before proceeding to the next one.

MOTIVATION

Challenge the students to find two different Ds and two different Gs on their instrument.

ASSESSMENT OF OBJECTIVES

1. Ask bass section to pizzicato high D and C♯ in third position.

2. Write ledger line notes on the board and ask viola, cello and bass students to identify note names.

3. Randomly call out the notes D and C♯ and ask students to put the correct number of fingers on the string.

4. Play a series of Ds and C♯s for the class and call on individual students to echo them.

CLOSURE

- Summarize new concepts.

- Remind students to continue pencil exercises but not to get the bow out.

- Remind students of correct position/posture while practicing.

- Remind students of proper left hand shape.

- Assign practice material based upon class performance.

UNIT 2 LESSON FIVE

OBJECTIVES	NATIONAL STANDARDS
At the end of instruction students should be able to:	
1. Place B on the fingerboard with the correct finger number.	2
2. Read B on the printed line of music.	5
3. Shift on bass.	2
4. Pizzicato all notes of the D Major scale by ear.	2
5. Pizzicato all notes of the D Major scale while reading a line of music.	2, 5
6. Define scale.	5

WARM-UP/REVIEW

• BOW BUILDERS ONE, TWO AND THREE

• Shoulder position for violin/viola

• Left hand *Workouts*

• Third position on bass

• D and C♯

STRATEGIES FOR TEACHING OBJECTIVES

1a. Ask students to place fingers on the note B.

1b. Check for proper left hand shape and finger placement.

1c. Ask students to pizzicato the note B.

2a. Identify B on the music staff in #28, *Let's Read "B"*.

2b. Play #28 pizzicato while saying/singing note names.

3a. Define shift for basses.

3b. Demonstrate the motion the hand must make to move from third position to first position.

3c. Ask basses to play two Ds, two quarter note rests, two C♯s, two quarter note rests, then shift to first position and play two Bs. Allow them to practice this several times by rote, both ascending and descending, until they feel comfortable making the shift.

4a. Call out note names for D, C♯ and B and ask students to pizzicato them.

4b. Play Listening Skills on TM pg. 65, examples 4–6.

5. Ask students to pizzicato #29, *Half Way Down*, #30, *Right Back Up*, #31, *Down the D Scale*, and #32, *Essential Elements Quiz* while saying/singing note names. Students should master each exercise before proceeding to the next one.

6. Read the definition of a scale out loud.

MOTIVATION

Play a scale and leave one note out. Ask students to name that note and play it on their own instrument.

ASSESSMENT OF OBJECTIVES

1. Ask students to close their eyes and place the correct finger on the fingerboard for the note B.

2. Ask students to count the number of Bs in #29, *Half Way Down.*

3. Ask basses to perform #30, *Right Back Up,* and observe their shifting technique.

4. Play notes from the D Major scale by rote and ask individual students to echo.

5. Ask the class to play #32, *Essential Elements Quiz – Up The D Scale* while saying/singing the notes. A sample playing quiz is available on pg. 124 based on the objectives identified on TM pg. 74.

6. Ask students to define a scale.

CLOSURE

- Summarize new concepts.

- Remind students to continue pencil exercises but not to get the bow out.

- Remind students of correct position/posture while practicing.

- Assign practice material based upon class performance.

UNIT 2 LESSON SIX

OBJECTIVES	NATIONAL STANDARDS
At the end of instruction students should be able to:	

1. Demonstrate the proper procedure for removing and replacing the bow in the case.
2. Identify the parts of the bow.   2
3. Demonstrate proper care of the bow.
4. Shape the right hand properly on the bow, BOW BUILDER FOUR.   2
5. Pizzicato various combinations of notes of the D Major scale while reading a printed line of music with increased proficiency.   2, 5
6. Create words by writing notes on a music staff.   4

WARM-UP/REVIEW

• *Listening Skills* on TM pg. 65

• Notes of the D Major scale

• BOW BUILDERS ONE, TWO AND THREE

• Shoulder position for violin/viola

• Left hand *Workouts*

STRATEGIES FOR TEACHING OBJECTIVES

1. Demonstrate the proper method for removing and replacing the bow in the case. Ask students to imitate. This is new for violins/violas, but review for cellos/basses.

2a. Ask students to study parts of the bow on pg. 2 in their books (TM pgs. 35–36).

2b. Hold a bow up in front of the class and point to the various parts of it.

3. Instruct students as to the delicate nature of the bow and how to handle it properly.

4. Follow steps 1–5 of BOW BUILDER FOUR (TM pg. 75) to instruct each section on how to hold the bow. Be sure students keep left hand holding the bow stick while shaping the right hand. STUDENTS SHOULD NOT TRY TO SHAPE THEIR HANDS ON THE BOW WITH ONLY ONE HAND HOLDING IT. Once hands are properly shaped, perform some of the same exercises previously done with the pencil, BOW BUILDER TWO.

5a. Ask students to say/sing note names in #33, *Song For Christine* and #34, *Natalie's Rose*.

5b. Ask students to pizzicato the exercises while saying/singing notes. Give special attention to the basses when they must shift.

5c. Perform these exercises with increasing levels of speed.

6. Ask students to complete #35, *Essential Creativity*. This can be done in individual sections while you assist other sections with refining their bow hand shape.

MOTIVATION

Demonstrate poor bow hand shape and call on students to correct it.

ASSESSMENT OF OBJECTIVES

1. Observe students putting their bows in cases. Remember, cellos and basses put bows in the case after the instrument.

2. Point to various parts of the bow and ask students to identify them.

3. Ask students to name the important elements of caring for the bow.

4. Observe students' bow hand shape and give verbal feedback.

5. Ask students to play #34, *Natalie's Rose,* one section at a time. While one group plays pizzicato the others will say/sing the names of the notes.

6. Ask each student to read one word that they created in #35. Check their books to see if they have the notes written correctly on the staff.

CLOSURE

- Summarize new concepts.

- Remind students to continue pencil exercises but not to get the bow out.

- Remind students of correct position/posture while practicing.

- Remind violin/viola students to practice putting the instrument in shoulder position for a few minutes during each practice session.

- Assign practice material based upon class performance

UNIT 2   LESSON SEVEN

OBJECTIVES	NATIONAL STANDARDS
At the end of instruction students should be able to:	
1. Name the small table-top spinning toy popular during Hanukkah.	9
2. Tighten and loosen the bow.	
3. Rosin the bow.	
4. Move the bow in both down and up directions.	2
5. Shadow bow with the rosin, BOW BUILDER FIVE.	2

WARM-UP/REVIEW

• Care of bow

• Parts of bow

• Shaping of right hand on the bow

• Right hand exercises

STRATEGIES FOR TEACHING OBJECTIVES

1. Have one student read the History section on pg. 12 out loud. Then ask the to class pizzicato #36, *Dreidel.*

2a. Instruct students to carefully pick up their bows.

2b. Ask students to look at how the bow hair and bow stick are very close together.

2c. While looking at the bow hair, have the students turn the bow screw clockwise and watch the hair move away from the stick. Make sure the bow stick always remains curved and is never straight.

2d. Ask students to observe the amount of space between the hair and the stick. Violins/violas should tighten the hair until there is enough space for their little finger to fit slightly between the hair and the stick; cellos/basses their first finger, but with more space so that the finger does not touch the hair or stick.

2e. Ask students to loosen the bow again. They should do this several times until you are sure they understand how tight and loose the bow hair should be.

2f. Remind students that the bow hair should always be loosened before putting the bow in the case.

3a. Ask students to get out their cake of rosin.

3b. While holding the rosin in the left hand, wrap the right hand all the way around the frog of the bow.

3c. Move the bow back and forth on the rosin, until a white powder appears on the bow hair. Note: If students have a new cake of rosin and bow hair without any rosin on it, special assistance will be needed by the teacher to "break in" the rosin. Also, synthetic hair will require students to rosin more frequently than horse hair.

4a. Have students place the bow on top of the rosin. (They may use either the early bow hold or the regular bow hold, whichever the teacher prefers.) Note: Because students are not really pressing down on the rosin, significant amounts of rosin should not accumulate on the bow.

4b. Without moving the rosin, have students slowly pull the bow to the right. Explain to them that this is called a "down bow".

4c. Without moving the rosin, have students slowly push the bow back to the left. Explain to them that this is called an "up bow".

4d. Allow students to experiment with a combination of down and up bows following the teacher by rote.

5. Ask students to bow #37–39, *Rosin Raps* on the rosin. They should say/sing "down" and "up" as indicated in their books. Students should master each exercise before proceeding to the next one.

MOTIVATION

Let each section demonstrate their bow hand shape to see how many "perfect" bow hands there are in each group.

ASSESSMENT OF OBJECTIVES

1. Ask students to name the small table-top spinning toy popular during Hanukkah.

2. Observe students as they tighten and loosen the bow.

3. Observe the amount of rosin on the students' bows.

4. Call out a series of down and up bows and have students respond by moving their bows in the appropriate direction.

5. Observe students performing #47, *Rosin Rap #3*. Evaluate students on their bow hand shape and on moving the bow at the appropriate time as indicated by quarter notes and quarter rests.

CLOSURE

- Summarize new concepts.

- Remind students of correct position/posture while practicing.

- Remind students not to put any additional rosin on their bows at home. (Since students have not really played with the bow yet, the rosin they put on in class is still there.)

- Remind students they may practice with the bow on the rosin but not to play with the bow on the instrument.

- Assign practice material based upon class performance.

UNIT 2 LESSON EIGHT

OBJECTIVES	NATIONAL STANDARDS
At the end of instruction students should be able to:	
1. Read note names on the music staff without the assistance of "Easy Read Notation."	5
2. Pizzicato in shoulder position for violin/viola.	2
3. Perform shadow bowing with increased proficiency.	2

WARM-UP/REVIEW

• Care of bow

• Parts of bow

• Shaping of right hand on the bow

• *Listening Skills* (TM pg. 65)

STRATEGIES FOR TEACHING OBJECTIVES

1a. Review the names of the lines and spaces for each clef.

1b. Ask students to write the note names in the box at top of pg. 14. Explain to students that note names will no longer appear in the note head so they must pay very close attention to the lines and spaces on the music staff.

2. Ask students to pizzicato #40, *Carolina Breeze*, #41, *Jingle Bells*, and #42, *Old MacDonald*. Violin/viola students should alternate the use of guitar and shoulder position. Students should master each exercise before proceeding to the next one.

3. Ask students to pick up their bows and carefully shape their hands on the bow. Practice rote bowing exercises while bowing on the rosin.

MOTIVATION

Play two notes. Ask the class to find those notes and play them on their instrument. Then select a student to write those notes on the board.

ASSESSMENT OF OBJECTIVES

1. Ask students to read the note names out loud in #41, *Jingle Bells*.

2. Ask students to perform #42, *Old MacDonald Had A Farm* with violins/violas playing pizzicato in shoulder position.

3. Ask students to echo a series of down and up bow patterns in 4/4 time.

CLOSURE

- Summarize new concepts.

- Remind students to practice shaping their hand on the bow but not to play with it on the instrument.

- Remind students to do left and right hand Work-outs daily.

- Remind students of correct position/posture while practicing.

- Remind violin/viola students to practice with their instrument in shoulder position as much as possible during each practice session.

- Assign practice material based upon class performance.

UNIT 2 LESSON NINE

OBJECTIVES	NATIONAL STANDARDS
At the end of instruction students should be able to:	
1. Name one fact about Mozart's life.	9
2. Recognize D Major key signature.	5
3. Pizzicato notes in D Major while reading notes on the music staff.	2
4. Compose two measures of music.	4

WARM-UP/REVIEW

• Shaping of right hand on the bow

• Shadow bowing, BOW BUILDER FIVE

• Left hand *Workouts*

• Pizzicato in shoulder position for violin/viola

• *Listening Skills* (TM pg. 65)

STRATEGIES FOR TEACHING OBJECTIVES

1a. Select one student to read the History section about Mozart out loud.

1b. Ask students to pizzicato #43, *A Mozart Melody*.

2a. Draw the D Major key signature on the board for each clef.

2b. Ask students to find D Major key signatures on other lines in the book.

3a. Direct students to say/sing note names before performing each exercise.

3b. Pizzicato #44, *Matthew's March* and #45, *Christopher's Tune*. Violin/viola students should be in shoulder position the majority of the time. Students should master each exercise before proceeding to the next one.

4. Ask students to pizzicato the first two measures of #46, *Essential Creativity*. Then ask them to complete the last two measures of the exercise using the rhythmic example provided.

MOTIVATION

Ask students to volunteer to play their compositions for the class.

ASSESSMENT OF OBJECTIVES

1. Ask students how old Mozart was when he performed in his first concert.

2. Ask students to name the sharps in the key of D Major.

3. Ask students to perform #45, *Christopher's Tune* while saying/singing note names.

4. Look at each student's book to see that they have completed #46.

CLOSURE

- Summarize new concepts.

- Remind students to do left and right hand *Workouts* daily.

- Remind students of correct position/posture while practicing.

- Remind violin/viola students to practice with their instrument in shoulder position as much as possible during each practice session.

- Assign practice material based upon class performance.

UNIT 3 LESSON ONE

OBJECTIVES	NATIONAL STANDARDS
At the end of instruction students should be able to:	
1. Play D and A strings with the bow by ear, BOW BUILDER SIX.	2
2. Define arco.	5
3. Play D and A strings with the bow while reading notes on the music staff.	2, 5

WARM-UP/REVIEW

• Tighten and loosen bow

• Shaping of right hand on bow

• BOW BUILDERS FOUR AND FIVE

• Moving bow in a down and up direction

STRATEGIES FOR TEACHING OBJECTIVES

1a. Ask students to shape bow hand properly using either the early bow hold or regular bow hold, whichever you prefer.

1b. Ask students to place instrument in proper playing position. Violin/viola students may place left hand on top of the instrument near the upper bout as in the picture (TM pg. 93). Do not let students play with a collapsed left wrist, even though they're only playing on open strings.

1c. Ask students to place bow on the string and relax their right hand and fingers.

1d. Allow students to experiment with moving the bow on the strings to produce a sound.

1e. Play Listening Skills (TM pg. 95) and ask students to echo.

2. Read definition of arco out loud.

3. Play #47, *Bow On The D String* and #48, *Bow On The A String* with the bow.

MOTIVATION

Let individual students play four-note open string patterns and ask the remainder of the class to echo.

ASSESSMENT OF OBJECTIVES

1. Play four-note patterns on D and A and ask individual students to echo.

2. Ask students to define arco.

3. Observe students playing #47, *Bow On The D String* and #48, *Bow On The A String* while looking at the book to see that they are following the printed line of music.

CLOSURE

- Summarize new concepts.

- Remind students of correct position/posture while practicing.

- Remind students to loosen bows and wipe off instruments.

- Remind students they may practice with the bow at home, but only on open strings.

- Assign practice material based upon class performance.

UNIT 3   LESSON TWO

OBJECTIVES	NATIONAL STANDARDS
At the end of instruction students should be able to:	
1. Raise and lower arm in proper direction to change between the D and A strings.	2
2. Play D and A strings with the bow parallel to the bridge while reading notes on the music staff with increased proficiency.	2, 5
3. Lift and reset the bow.	2
4. Echo fingered note patterns of the D Major scale while bowing, BOW BUILDER SEVEN.	2

WARM-UP/REVIEW

• Shaping of right hand on bow

• Moving bow in a down and up direction

• *Listening Skills* (TM pg. 95)

STRATEGIES FOR TEACHING OBJECTIVES

1a. Ask students to place bow on the D string.

1b. Without making any sound, have students rock the bow back and forth between the D and the A strings.

1c. Observe students' shoulders to be sure they remain relaxed.

1d. Assign students to memorize the guidelines for raising and lowering arm (TM pg. 98).

1e. Ask students to play #49, *Raise And Lower,* and make sure they raise and lower their arms in the appropriate direction as indicated in their music. Note: Cellists will be raising their arms when everyone else is lowering theirs and vice versa.

2a. Ask students to place the bow on the D string about halfway between the fingerboard and bridge.

2b. Have students pull a down bow, trying to keep the same distance between the bridge and fingerboard.

2c. Repeat the same procedure with an up bow.

2d. Ask students to play #50, *Teeter Totter* and #51, *Mirror Image.*

3a. Read the definition of a bow lift out loud.

3b. Direct students to do some bow lifts by rote, reminding them to keep their bow hand shape properly formed and relaxed at all times.

3c. Ask students to perform #52, *A Strand of D 'N' A.*

4a. Ask students to put down the correct number of fingers for the note G (F♯ for basses).

4b. While holding fingers down, students carefully pull the bow across the string. Starting with the note G, have them continue doing this as they lift fingers in a descending scale pattern. Repeat the same procedure starting on high D.

4c. Let students experiment with playing various notes with the bow.

4d. Play BOW BUILDER SEVEN (TM pg. 102) and ask students to echo various combinations of notes from the D Major scale.

MOTIVATION

Challenge each instrument section to see who can pull the straightest bow.

ASSESSMENT OF OBJECTIVES

1. Have one section play #49, *Raise And Lower* arco and observe their bow arms. The remainder of the class should be playing pizzicato.

2. Ask students to play #53, *Essential Elements Quiz – Olympic Challenge* in small groups. A sample playing quiz is available on page 125 based on the objectives identified on TM pg. 101.

3. Observe students to see that they are lifting the bow as indicated when they play #52, *Strand of D'N'A*.

4. Teacher plays four-note patterns and asks individual students to echo them.

CLOSURE

• Summarize new concepts.

• Remind students of correct position/posture while practicing.

• Remind students to loosen bows and wipe off instruments.

• Assign practice material based upon class performance.

UNIT 3 LESSON THREE

<table>
<tr><td>OBJECTIVES</td><td>NATIONAL STANDARDS</td></tr>
</table>

At the end of instruction students should be able to:
1. Echo fingered note patterns of the D Major scale while bowing with increased proficiency. — 2
2. List the four steps in practicing for success.
3. Play notes on the D string (also open G string for bass) arco while reading notes on the music staff. — 2, 5

WARM-UP/REVIEW

- Bow hand shape
- BOW BUILDER SEVEN
- Bowing parallel to the bridge
- Bow lift

STRATEGIES FOR TEACHING OBJECTIVES

1a. Play various patterns of the D Major scale and ask students to echo.

1b. Let individual students create four-note patterns and ask the class to echo.

1c. Ask students to play the D Major scale in various combinations of quarter notes and quarter rests.

2. Read and discuss the four steps for practicing for success.

3. Ask students to play #54, *Bowing "G,"* #55, *Back and Forth,* #56, *Down and Up,* #57, *Tribal Lament,* #58, *Bowing "D,"* #59, *Little Steps,* and #60, *Elevator Down,* incorporating the four steps for practicing on each line. Students should master each exercise before proceeding to the next one.

MOTIVATION

Ask students to count off in groups of four. As you call out a number, students with the corresponding number can demonstrate practicing for success for the remainder of the class.

ASSESSMENT OF OBJECTIVES

1. Play four-note echo patterns and ask individual students to echo them.

2. Without using their books, ask each section to name one step to practicing for success.

3. Ask students to play #60, *Elevator Down*. Small groups play arco, while the others play pizzicato.

CLOSURE

- Summarize new concepts.

- Remind students of correct position/posture while practicing.

- Remind students to loosen bows and wipe off instruments.

- Assign practice material based upon class performance.

UNIT 3 LESSON FOUR

OBJECTIVES	NATIONAL STANDARDS
At the end of instruction students should be able to:	
1. Echo fingered note patterns in the D Major scale while bowing with increased proficiency.	2
2. Play the D Major scale arco while reading notes on the music staff.	2, 5
3. Play C♯ on the A string for bass.	2

WARM-UP/REVIEW

• BOW BUILDERS SIX AND SEVEN

• Shaping left hand

• Bowing parallel to the bridge

• Bowing notes on D string (open G for bass) while reading notes on the music staff

• Four steps to practicing for success

STRATEGIES FOR TEACHING OBJECTIVES

1a. Play various patterns of the D Major scale and ask students to echo them.

1b. Make up additional combinations with increasing levels of difficulty.

2. Ask students to play #61, *Elevator Up,* #62, *Down the D Major Scale,* and #63, *Scale Similator* using the four steps to practicing for success on each exercise. Students should master each exercise before proceeding to the next one.

3a. Ask violins, violas and cellos to complete the special exercise on pg. 19 in their book.

3b. Ask basses to place four fingers on the A string for C♯ as indicated in the diagram on pg. 19 in their book.

3c. While holding their fingers down, ask them to pizzicato the new note C♯.

3d. Ask bass students to play #65, *Let's Read "C♯".*

3e. Ask entire class to play #65.

MOTIVATION

Ask students to create words using note names from the D Major scale, then have them play that word on their instrument.

ASSESSMENT OF OBJECTIVES

1. Play four-note echo patterns and ask individual students to echo them.

2. Ask students to play #64, *Essential Elements Quiz – The D Major Scale*. One section plays arco while the others play pizzicato. A sample playing quiz is available on pg. 126 based on the objectives identified on TM pg. 110.

3. Ask the bass section to play #65, *Let's Read "C♯"* arco while the remainder of the class plays pizzicato.

CLOSURE

- Summarize new concepts.

- Remind students of correct position/posture while practicing.

- Remind students to loosen bows and wipe off instruments.

- Assign practice material based upon class performance.

UNIT 3 LESSON FIVE

OBJECTIVES	NATIONAL STANDARDS
At the end of instruction students should be able to:	
1. Identify the flag on one eighth note and the beam on two eighth notes.	5
2. Count, clap and shadow bow eighth and quarter notes.	2
3. Play eighth and quarter notes in various combinations of pitches from the D Major scale.	2
4. Define Andante, Moderato and Allegro.	5

WARM-UP/REVIEW

• Acceptable right and left hand position

• Echo patterns of the D Major scale

• Four steps to practicing for success

STRATEGIES FOR TEACHING OBJECTIVES

1. Ask students to look in the box at the top of page 20 and describe the difference between a flag and a beam.

2a. Ask students to tap a steady beat while counting out loud.

2b. Ask students to clap quarter notes.

2c. Ask students to clap eighth notes.

2d. Ask students to shadow bow (see TM pg. 81) eighth notes, while tapping a quarter note beat.

3a. Using the four-step method described on TM pg. 113, have students perform #66, *Rhythm Rap*. Remind them to use less bow on the eighth note than they do on the quarter notes. Students then perform #67, *Pepperoni Pizza*.

3b. Using the four-step method again, ask students to perform #68, *Rhythm Rap*.

3c. Students perform #69, *D Major Scale Up*, #70, *Hot Cross Buns*, and #71, *Au Clair De La Lune*. Approach each exercise by using the four steps to practicing for success on student book pg. 18. Students should master each exercise before proceeding to the next one.

4a. Ask individual students to read definitions of the three tempo markings out loud.

4b. Ask students to clap a steady beat at different speeds corresponding to the tempo markings.

MOTIVATION

Using combinations of quarter and eighth notes, ask students to create their own rhythms for the D Major scale.

ASSESSMENT OF OBJECTIVES

1. Students draw one single eighth note with a flag and two and/or four eighth notes with a beam on the board.

2. Ask individual sections to shadow bow eight notes, while tapping quarters. Observe their bows to see that they are counting accurately.

3. Observe bowing while students perform #71, *Au Claire De La Lune.*

4. Ask various students to define Andante, Moderato and Allegro.

CLOSURE

- Summarize new concepts.

- Remind students of correct position/posture while practicing.

- Remind students to loosen bows and wipe off instruments.

- Assign practice material based upon class performance.

UNIT 3 LESSON SIX

OBJECTIVES	NATIONAL STANDARDS

At the end of instruction students should be able to:

1. Count and perform increasingly complex combinations of quarter and eighth notes in 4/4 time.	2
2. Define what 2 and 4 stand for in 2/4 time signature.	5
3. Demonstrate the two-beat conducting pattern.	2
4. Count and perform notes of the D Major scale in a 2/4 time signature.	2, 5
5. Play 1st and 2nd endings.	2, 5

WARM-UP/REVIEW

• Acceptable right and left hand position

• Flags and beams

• Counting eighth notes

STRATEGIES FOR TEACHING OBJECTIVES

1a. Using the four-step method described on TM pg. 113, have students perform #72, *Rhythm Rap*. Remind them to use less bow on the eighth note than they do on the quarter notes.

1b. Ask students to pizzicato and shadow bow #73, *Buckeye Salute*. Then have the students play it arco.

2a. Ask students to read the explanation of the 2/4 time signature on pg. 21.

2b. Compare the 2/4 time signature to a 4/4 time signature.

3. Have students practice the two-beat conducting pattern as illustrated in the book.

4a. Using the four-step method, ask students to perform #74, *Rhythm Rap*.

4b. Students perform #75, *Two By Two*.

5a. Read the definition of first and second endings to the class.

5b. Draw a diagram on the board with arrows pointing to the first and second endings.

5c. Ask students to identify in their books the first and second endings in #76, *Essential Elements Quiz – For Pete's Sake*.

MOTIVATION

Select students to conduct the class playing one of the 2/4 lines.

ASSESSMENT OF OBJECTIVES

1. Ask students to bow the rhythm in #73, *Buckeye Salute* in the air and visually assess the accuracy of the bow direction for each student.

2. Ask individual students to explain the 2/4 time signature.

3. Observe students conducting a two-beat pattern.

4. Students play #76 while tapping a steady beat. A sample playing quiz is available on pg. 127 based on the objectives identified on TM pg. 118.

5. Ask students to play only the first ending, then only the second ending in #76.

CLOSURE

• Summarize new concepts.

• Remind students of correct position/posture while practicing.

• Remind students to loosen bows and wipe off instruments.

• Assign practice material based upon class performance.

UNIT 3   LESSON SEVEN

OBJECTIVES	NATIONAL STANDARDS
At the end of instruction students should be able to:	
1. Count and perform half notes and half rests while keeping a steady beat.	2, 5
2. Move the bow at a slower speed to perform half notes.	2
3. Identify and observe an enclosed repeat sign.	5
4. Pizzicato with the fourth finger of the left hand.	2

WARM-UP/REVIEW

• Acceptable right and left hand position

• 2/4 time

• Counting eighth notes

STRATEGIES FOR TEACHING OBJECTIVES

1a. Ask students to read the definition of half note and half rest on pg. 22.

1b. Ask students to shadow bow #77, *Rhythm Rap,* then play it on open D.

2a. Ask students to shadow bow #78, *At Pierrot's Door.* When they come to the half notes they should say "slow bow," saying each word with a quarter note value.

2b. Students play #78, *The Half Counts* and #80, *Grandparent's Day* arco, being sure to move their bows more slowly on the half notes than on the quarter notes.

3a. Ask students to read the definition of enclosed repeat sign on pg. 22.

3b. Ask students to find the enclosed repeat sign in #81, *Michael Row The Boat Ashore.*

3c. Ask students to say the note names as they point to them in the book, then play the line as printed.

4a. Have students pizzicato open strings with the fourth finger of their left hand.

4b. Ask students to play #82, *Texas Two-String.* Make sure they are using the fourth finger of their left hand, not their right hand, to pluck the string.

MOTIVATION

Challenge the students to see who can play the largest number of counts in a down bow.

ASSESSMENT OF OBJECTIVES

1. Have one section clap half notes while the other sections clap steady quarter notes.

2. Evaluate students' different bow speeds for quarter notes and half notes while playing #81.

3. Ask students to describe the characteristics of an enclosed repeat sign.

4. Teacher observes the students' left hand for proper playing position as students play #82.

CLOSURE

- Summarize new concepts.

- Remind students of correct position/posture while practicing.

- Remind students to loosen bows and wipe off instruments.

- Assign practice material based upon class performance.

UNIT 3 LESSON EIGHT

OBJECTIVES	NATIONAL STANDARDS
At the end of instruction students should be able to:	
1. Play G and A in III position for bass.	2
2. Play fourth finger on the D string for violin/viola.	2
3. Identify Beethoven as a great German composer.	9

WARM-UP/REVIEW

• Acceptable right and left hand position

• Half notes and half rests

• Counting eighth notes

• Left hand pizzicato

STRATEGIES FOR TEACHING OBJECTIVES

1a. Ask bass students to place their hands in III position on the G string.

1b. Ask them to move their hands straight across to the D string.

1c. Ask them to pizzicato the note A with all four fingers down on the D string and compare it with the open A string.

1d. Ask bass students to pizzicato the note G with only one finger down and compare it with the open G string.

2a. Ask violin/viola students to put three fingers down on the D string and evaluate each student's left hand shape.

2b. Ask them to put their fourth finger down on the string, then lift it up and down several times.

2c. While keeping their fourth fingers down, have students pizzicato the note A and compare it with the open A string.

2d. Ask students to play #83, *Four By Four*, #84, *4th Finger Marathon*, #85, *High Flying*, and #86, *Elements Quiz – Ode to Joy*. Students should master each exercise before proceeding to the next one.

3. Have one student read the History section about Beethoven to the class.

MOTIVATION

Ask for volunteers to play #86, *Ode To Joy* for the class.

ASSESSMENT OF OBJECTIVES

1. Basses play #83, and teacher observes their left hands for correct fingerings and positions.

2. Violins/violas play #86 arco while the remainder of the class plays pizzicato. A sample playing quiz is available on pg. 128 based on the objectives identified on TM pg. 128.

3. Ask students to name the country Beethoven represents.

CLOSURE

- Summarize new concepts.

- Remind students of correct position/posture while practicing.

- Remind students to loosen bows and wipe off instruments.

- Assign practice material based upon class performance.

UNIT 4 LESSON ONE

OBJECTIVES	NATIONAL STANDARDS
At the end of instruction students should be able to:	
1. Define three elements of concert etiquette.	
2. Perform a *round* in two parts.	2
3. Define *chord* and *harmony*.	5
4. Perform an orchestra arrangement.	2

WARM-UP/REVIEW

• Acceptable right and left hand position

• Eighth, quarter and half notes

• #87, *Scale Warm-up*

STRATEGIES FOR TEACHING OBJECTIVES

1a. Discuss the important elements of a public performance with the class.

1b. Ask students to read and discuss their responsibilities in contributing to the success of a performance.

2a. Ask the class to play #88, *Frere Jacques* in unison.

2b. Discuss the important elements in performing a round.

2c. Ask students to point to the numbers 1 and 2 in #88 on pg. 24 in their books.

2d. Divide the class into two groups and have them perform a round.

3. Read and discuss the definition of chord and harmony.

4a. Explain parts A and B to the class in #89, *Bile 'Em Cabbage Down*.

4b. Ask all students to perform part A.

4c. Ask all students to perform part B.

4d. Ask students to perform #89 in various combinations of A and B parts.

MOTIVATION

Let students play #89, *Bile 'Em Cabbage Down* by using the A string as a drone, thus creating double stops.

ASSESSMENT OF OBJECTIVES

1. Ask students to write a paragraph describing proper concert etiquette.

2. Divide students into small groups and assign them a part to play in #88, *Frère Jacques*.

3. Ask students to identify a harmony part in their books.

4. Divide the class into groups of four and ask each group to perform #89 for the other class members.

CLOSURE

- Summarize new concepts.

- Remind students of correct position/posture while practicing.

- Remind students of proper concert etiquette.

- Assign practice material based upon class performance.

UNIT 4 LESSON TWO

OBJECTIVES	NATIONAL STANDARDS
At the end of instruction students should be able to:	
1. Perform a round with increased proficiency.	2
2. Name two art forms that are used in an operetta.	8
3. Perform orchestra arrangements with increased proficiency.	2

WARM-UP/REVIEW

• Acceptable right and left hand position

• Concert etiquette

• Chord, harmony

STRATEGIES FOR TEACHING OBJECTIVES

1a. Perform #90, *English Round* in unison. Make sure students are subdividing in the first two measures.

1b. Divide the class into two groups and have them perform #90 as a round.

2. Read and discuss the various elements used in creating an operetta.

3a. Rehearse the parts marked A in #91, *Lightly Row* and #92, *Can-Can* in unison.

3b. Rehearse the B parts for #91 and #92.

3c. Divide the class into the appropriate groups and rehearse the arrangements with both parts.

MOTIVATION

Let students see how fast they can play #93, *Can-Can*.

ASSESSMENT OF OBJECTIVES

1. Ask students to perform #90, *English Round* in small groups for the class.

2. Ask students to list two art forms that are used in an operetta.

3. Ask students to write a self assessment of their performance in the ensembles. Ask them to list their strong points, as well as suggest areas of improvement.

CLOSURE

- Summarize new concepts.

- Remind students of correct position/posture while practicing.

- Remind students of proper concert etiquette.

- Assign practice material based upon class performance.

UNIT 4 LESSON THREE

OBJECTIVES	NATIONAL STANDARDS
At the end of instruction students should be able to:	
1. Recognize G Major key signature.	5
2. Define ledger lines for violin.	5
3. Play the pitches C, B and A on the G string for violin, viola and cello.	2
4. Play the pitch G on the E string and pitches C and B on the A string for bass.	2

WARM-UP/REVIEW

• Acceptable right and left hand position

• Third position on the D string for bass

• Fourth finger on the D string for violin/viola

STRATEGIES FOR TEACHING OBJECTIVES

1. Ask students to compare the G Major and D Major key signatures.

2. Ask violin students to read the definition of ledger lines on pg. 26 in their book.

3a. Demonstrate playing on the G string for violins, violas and cellos and show students how to slow their bow speed to produce a good tone.

3b. Demonstrate the pitches C, B and A on the G string for violins, violas and cello, and then ask students to find and play these on their instruments.

4a. Demonstrate the pitch G on the E string for basses and ask students to find and play G on their instrument.

4b. Demonstrate the pitches C and B on the A string for basses and ask students to find and play them on their instrument

4c. Play *Listening Skills* (TM pg. 139) for all students to echo.

4d. Practice #93, *Let's Read "G,"* #94, *Let's Read "C,"* #95, *Let's Read "E,"* and #96, *Let's Read "A,"* with all instruments. Students should master each exercise before proceeding to the next one.

MOTIVATION

Have a contest between sections to see who has the best overall left hand position.

ASSESSMENT OF OBJECTIVES

1. Ask students to describe how the G Major scale is similar to and different from the D Major scale.

2. Ask violin students to identify ledger lines in their music.

3. Ask violin, viola and cello students to play #96, *Let's Read "A"* and observe their left hands for correct fingerings and playing position.

4. Ask bass students to play #96 and observe their left hands for correct fingerings and playing position.

CLOSURE

- Summarize new concepts.

- Remind students that the larger the string the slower the bow must move to produce a good tone.

- Remind students of correct position/posture while practicing.

- Remind students to loosen bows and wipe off instruments.

- Assign practice material based upon class performance.

UNIT 4 LESSON FOUR

OBJECTIVES	NATIONAL STANDARDS
At the end of instruction students should be able to:	
1. Identify G string pitches on the staff.	5
2. Demonstrate fourth finger D on the G string (violin/viola).	2
3. Identify and define Common Time.	5
4. Perform in G Major with eighth, quarter, and half notes.	2

WARM-UP/REVIEW

• G Major key signature

• Bowing parallel to the bridge while playing the G Major scale

STRATEGIES FOR TEACHING OBJECTIVES

1a. Ask students to name the notes in #97, *Walking Around,* before playing.

1b. Ask students to write the note names in their books for #98, *G Major Scale,* and then perform the line.

2a. Ask violin/viola students to practice sliding their fourth finger on the G string a whole step away from their third finger. Be sure to adjust elbow forward.

2b. Ask violin/viola students to play the first five notes of the G Major scale beginning on their G string and match their fourth finger D on the G string with their open D string.

2c. Rehearse #99, *Fourth Finger D* checking the intonation of the fingered note carefully.

3a. Ask students to write the Common Time signature on the board.

3b. Ask students to practice conducting a four-beat pattern while counting.

3c. Ask students to practice #100, *Low Down.*

4. Ask students to count and tap #101, *Baa Baa Black Sheep.* Ask students to say/sing note names before playing it arco.

MOTIVATION

Play fingered Ds on the G string with some in tune and some out of tune. Ask students to count the number in tune and then play that number of fingered Ds on their instrument.

ASSESSMENT OF OBJECTIVES

1. Ask students to read the note names out loud in #102, *Essential Elements Quiz – This Old Man.*

2. Ask violin students to perform the first two measures in #102 and observe their left hands.

3. Ask students to find a Common Time signature on another page in their books.

4. Ask students to play #102, *Essential Elements Quiz – This Old Man.* A sample playing quiz is available on pg. 129 based on the objectives identified on TM pg. 148.

CLOSURE

- Summarize new concepts.

- Remind violin/viola students to listen carefully to their fourth finger D on the G string to make sure it is in tune when practicing.

- Assign practice material based upon class performance.

UNIT 4 LESSON FIVE

OBJECTIVES	NATIONAL STANDARDS
At the end of instruction students should be able to:	
1. Define 3/4 time signature.	5
2. Demonstrate a three-beat conducting pattern.	2
3. Count and perform dotted half notes.	2
4. Count and perform music in a 3/4 time signature.	2
5. Play B in II1/2 position for bass.	2

WARM-UP/REVIEW

• Acceptable right and left hand position

• Bow speed

STRATEGIES FOR TEACHING OBJECTIVES

1a. Ask students to read the explanation of the 3/4 time signature at the top of pg. 28.

1b. Compare the 3/4 time signature with the 4/4 and 2/4 time signatures.

2. Ask students to practice the three-beat conducting pattern as illustrated in the book.

3. Ask students to pull their bows on the D string while counting three quarter note beats.

4a. Ask students to clap and shadow bow #103, *Rhythm Rap*.

4b. Ask students to perform #104, *Counting Threes*, and #105, D *Major Scale in Threes*. Approach each exercise by counting aloud, playing pizzicato, shadow bowing and playing arco. Students should master each exercise before proceeding to the next one.

5a. Ask bass students to find D and C♯ in third position.

5b. Basses play each note four times.

5c. Ask basses to find the B in II 1/2 position by sliding their hand slightly toward the scroll.

5d. Ask bass students to play D, C#, and B by rote a few times. Then continue with the entire class playing #106, *French Folk Song*, and #107, *Essential Elements Quiz – Sailor's Song*.

MOTIVATION

Ask individual students to conduct selected exercises in 3/4 time.

ASSESSMENT OF OBJECTIVES

1. Ask various students to explain the 3/4 time signature.

2. Observe all students conducting the three-beat pattern.

3. Ask students to play a D Major scale with dotted quarter notes while counting to three on each note.

4. Students perform #107, *Essential Elements Quiz – Sailor's Song* while keeping a steady beat. A sample playing quiz is available on pg. 130 based on the objectives identified on TM pg. 153.

5. While the class performs #106, *French Folk Song,* observe the basses closely to see if they are shifting correctly for the B in II 1/2 position.

CLOSURE

- Summarize new concepts.

- Remind students of correct position/posture while practicing.

- Remind students to loosen bows and wipe off instruments.

- Assign practice material based upon class performance.

UNIT 4   LESSON SIX

OBJECTIVES	NATIONAL STANDARDS
At the end of instruction students should be able to:	
1. Define and perform a tie.	2, 5
2. Define a slur.	5
3. Play two-note slurs on one string.	2
4. Play two-note slurs with string crossings.	2

WARM-UP/REVIEW

• Slow and fast bow speeds

• G string notes

• Counting dotted half notes

STRATEGIES FOR TEACHING OBJECTIVES

1a. Read aloud the definition of a tie on pg. 29.

1b. Ask students to see how many counts they can "tie" together in one bow.

1c. Ask students to count a specific number of counts in one bow.

1d. Play #108, *Fit To Be Tied.*

2. Read aloud the definition of a slur.

3a. Ask students to sustain the open D string while lifting their first finger up and down as many times as possible, similar to a trill.

3b. Ask students to see how many first finger Es they can play in one down bow, then one up bow.

3c. Ask students to repeat the process with different notes. For example, while sustaining an E on the D string, make the finger playing F♯ go up and down as many times as possible.

3d. Ask students to play one D and one E with a down bow, then repeat on an up bow.

3e. Ask students to say or sing #109, *Stop And Go* while bowing in the air.

3f. Ask students to perform #110, *Slurring Along,* #111, *Smooth Sailing,* and #112, *D Major Slurs.* Students should master each exercise before proceeding to the next one.

4a. Demonstrate slurring open D and A strings and ask students to imitate.

4b. Ask students to perform #113, *Crossing Strings,* #114, *Gliding Bows,* and #115, *Upside Down.* Students should master each exercise before proceeding to the next one.

MOTIVATION

Challenge students to see how many notes they can play on one bow.

ASSESSMENT OF OBJECTIVES

1. Ask students to define and play an example of a tie.

2. Ask students to define a slur.

3. Ask students to perform #112 and evaluate their slurs.

4. Ask students to perform #115 and evaluate their slurred string crossings.

CLOSURE

- Summarize new concepts.

- Remind students to slur carefully when practicing at home.

- Assign practice material based upon class performance.

UNIT 4 LESSON SEVEN

OBJECTIVES	NATIONAL STANDARDS
At the end of instruction students should be able to:	
1. Define and play an upbeat.	2, 5
2. Describe the unique sounds of Latin American music and give examples of instruments used to play Latin music.	9
3. Define D.C. al Fine and explain the form of a piece with a D.C. al Fine.	2, 5
4. Perform an orchestra arrangement.	2

WARM-UP/REVIEW

• Counting quarter and eighth notes in 3/4 time as in #103, *Counting Threes*

• Bowing parallel to the bridge while playing the G Major scale

STRATEGIES FOR TEACHING OBJECTIVES

1a. Read aloud definition of upbeat.

1b. Ask students to identify the upbeat in #116, *Song for Maria* and the upbeats in #118, *Firoliralera.*

1c. Rehearse #116, with the upbeat beginning on an up bow.

2. Read and discuss the history of Latin American Music on pg. 30.

3. Ask students to read aloud the definition of D.C. al Fine before explaining the form of #117, *Banana Boat Song.* Ask students to point to the Fine.

4a. Ask students to play part A in #118, *Firoliralera.*

4b. Ask students to play part B.

4c. Once both parts have been learned, divide the students into various groups to perform #118.

MOTIVATION

Add an accompaniment to #117, *Banana Boat Song* with drums, maracas, and/or claves.

ASSESSMENT OF OBJECTIVES

1. Ask students to define upbeat and play #116, *Song for Maria.*

2. Ask students to name the countries that contribute to Latin American music.

3. Ask students to define D.C. al Fine.

4. Listen to students perform #118, *Firoliralera* in small groups.

CLOSURE

- Summarize new concepts.

- Remind violin/viola students to listen carefully to their fourth finger D on the G string to make sure it is in tune when practicing.

- Assign practice material based upon class performance.

UNIT 4 LESSON EIGHT

OBJECTIVES	NATIONAL STANDARDS
At the end of instruction students should be able to:	
1. Perform exercises in the key of G Major in increasingly difficult technical sequences.	2
2. Slur three quarter notes on one bow.	2
3. Name one country where Far Eastern music originated.	9

WARM-UP/REVIEW

• G Major key signature

• G Major scale

• Upbeat

• Slurs

STRATEGIES FOR TEACHING OBJECTIVES

1a. Ask students to study the various time signatures found in #119–124, *Skill Builders*.

1b. Approach each exercise with the following sequence:

   • Count and tap

   • Shadow bow

   • Play pizzicato

   • Play as written

2a. Play a two note slur.

2b. Have students add one more note to the slur.

2c. Play the notes G, F♯ and E by rote with a 3 note slur.

2d. Play #123.

3. Read aloud the History of Far Eastern music on pg. 31. Discuss some of the countries in which Far Eastern music would be heard.

MOTIVATION

Ask students to write a simple four-bar melody which has three note slurs in the key of G Major.

ASSESSMENT OF OBJECTIVES

1. Ask students to perform #125, *Jingli Nona* in small groups.

2. Ask students to perform #123, and observe their bows.

3. Ask students to name a country where they would hear Far Eastern music.

CLOSURE

- Summarize new concepts.

- Remind students to always carefully count and tap the beats when practicing.

- Assign practice material based upon class performance.

UNIT 5 LESSON ONE

OBJECTIVES	NATIONAL STANDARDS
At the end of instruction students should be able to:	
1. Play F-natural on the D string.	2
2. Identify a natural sign.	5
3. Define half step and whole step.	5

WARM-UP/REVIEW

• Left hand shape

• Bowing parallel to the bridge

STRATEGIES FOR TEACHING OBJECTIVES

1a. Ask violin/viola students to hold their hands up and show the low second finger pattern.

1b. Ask all students to place their left hand on the fingerboard and tap their second finger while keeping their other fingers on the string.

1c. Ask all students to slide their second finger on the string between their first and third fingers.

1d. Ask students to hold first and second fingers on the D string and tap their other fingers.

1e. Play *Listening Skills* (TM pg. 173) and ask students to echo.

1f. Play #126, *Let's Read "F,"* emphasizing intonation of F-natural.

2. Ask students to draw natural signs on the board.

3a. Read aloud the definitions of half step and whole step to the class.

3b. Play #127, *Half-Steppin' and Whole Steppin'*, #128, *Spy Guy*, and #129, *Minor Details*. Students should master each exercise before proceeding to the next one.

MOTIVATION

Challenge students to find another sharp note on their instruments and make it a natural.

ASSESSMENT OF OBJECTIVES

1. Ask students to perform #128, *Spy Guy* and listen to F-naturals.

2. Ask students to count the number of natural signs on student book page 32.

3. Ask students to write the definition of half step and whole step.

CLOSURE

- Summarize new concepts.

- Remind students to watch carefully for F-naturals and F♯s.

- Assign practice material based upon class performance.

UNIT 5 LESSON TWO

OBJECTIVES	NATIONAL STANDARDS
At the end of instruction students should be able to:	
1. Identify and play C-natural on the A string.	2, 5
2. Define chromatics.	5

WARM-UP/REVIEW

• Low-second finger pattern on the D string (violin/viola)

• F-natural and F♯ on the D string

• C♯ on the A string

STRATEGIES FOR TEACHING OBJECTIVES

1a. Ask violin/viola students to show their low second-finger pattern by holding their left hand in the air with their first and second fingers touching and their third and fourth fingers spread apart.

1b. Ask them to place their first finger on the A string. While holding that finger down, have them tap and slide their second finger.

1c. Play *Listening Skills* (TM pg. 179) and ask students to echo.

1d. Rehearse #130, *Let's Read "C"* and #131, *Half Step And Whole Step Review*. Students should master #130 before proceeding to #131.

2a. Ask students to read the definition of chromatics on pg. 33.

2b. Rehearse #132, *Chromatic Moves*, #133, *The Stetson Special*, and #134, *Bluebird's Song*. Point out that #134, *Bluebird's Song*, is a Texas folk song. Discuss with the students the official song of their state.

MOTIVATION

Ask students to make up their own pattern of notes incorporating B, C-natural, C♯, and fingered D for their classmates to echo.

ASSESSMENT OF OBJECTIVES

1. Ask students to play #131, *Half Step And Whole Step Review*. Visually evaluate fingerings, violin/viola finger patterns, and intonation.

2. Ask students to define chromatics. Then have them circle all chromatic notes in #312, *Chromatic Moves*.

CLOSURE

- Summarize new concepts.

- Remind students to listen carefully to their C-naturals when they are practicing.

- Assign practice material based upon class performance.

UNIT 5 LESSON THREE

OBJECTIVES	NATIONAL STANDARDS
At the end of instruction students should be able to:	
1. Play in the key of C Major.	5
2. Play second finger B and fourth finger C in second position for basses.	2
3. Define and perform a duet.	2, 5
4. Perform a line in C Major with an upbeat.	2
5. Identify one characteristic of nationalistic music.	9

WARM-UP/REVIEW

• Low second finger pattern on the D string for violin/viola

• Low second finger pattern on the A string for violin/viola

• F-natural and C-natural on the A string

• Definition of a round

STRATEGIES FOR TEACHING OBJECTIVES

1a. Ask violin/viola students to show their low-second finger pattern by holding their left hand in the air with their first and second fingers touching, and their third and fourth fingers spread apart.

1b. Have students sustain and tune F-natural and C-natural.

2a. Demonstrate for basses how to play B and C in second position and ask basses to imitate.

2b. Sustain and tune each of the pitches in exercise #135, *C Major Scale – Round*. Then skip to #137, *Oak Hollow*, which uses all the notes of the scale, but in a different sequence.

3a. Read and discuss with students the definition of the term duet.

3b. Allow students to select which part, A or B, they would like to play for exercise #136, *Split Decision*.

4. Review the definition of an upbeat and demonstrate its application in #138, *A-Tisket, A-Tasket*. Ask students to perform #138.

5. Discuss the concept of nationalism in music as you rehearse #139, *Essential Elements Quiz – Russian Folk Tune*. Illustrate nationalism by playing an excerpt from *The Moldau*.

MOTIVATION

Ask students to transpose and play #106, *French Folk Song* in the key of C Major. Tell them to begin and end the melody on C.

ASSESSMENT OF OBJECTIVES

1. Ask students to play #139, *Essential Elements Quiz – Russian Folk Tune*. Evaluate fingerings and violin/viola finger patterns. A sample playing quiz is available on pg. 131 based on the objectives identified on TM pg. 188.

2. Ask bass students to perform #139 arco while the remainder of the class plays pizzicato. Carefully observe left hands to see if they are shifting correctly and playing the correct fingerings.

3. Ask students to define duet. Then listen to them play #136 in small groups.

4. Count the beat out loud and ask students to begin line #138 on the correct beat.

5. Ask students to name a characteristic of nationalism in music.

CLOSURE

• Summarize new concepts.

• Remind students to listen carefully to their C Major scale frequently so that it is mastered as well as their familiar D and G Major scales.

• Assign practice material based upon class performance.

UNIT 5 LESSON FOUR

OBJECTIVES	NATIONAL STANDARDS
At the end of instruction students should be able to:	
1. Perform F♯ and C-natural in alternating sequences.	2
2. Describe the difference between Theme and Variations and Rounds.	6
3. Create different rhythms for a melody.	3

WARM-UP/REVIEW

• Definition of upbeat.

• C-natural on the A string

• Second and third positions on the G string on the bass

• Definition of round

STRATEGIES FOR TEACHING OBJECTIVES

1. Ask violin/viola students to hold their left hands in the air and demonstrate the low-second finger pattern and the high-second finger pattern. Perform #140, *Bingo* and point out that it uses both finger patterns.

2a. Read the History section about the life and times of the English composer Thomas Tallis. Ask students to play #141, *Tallis Canon – Round.*

2b. Describe the differences between a round and a theme and variations. Ask students to explain how Variation I in #142, *Variations on A Familiar Song* is similar but different from the theme.

2c. Give students an opportunity to create and play in class their own variations. Ask students what well-known melody *(Skip to My Lou)* is the basis for #142. Suggest to students that they first change the bowings and/or rhythms.

3. Give students the opportunity to create and play their own rhythmic variations of #143, *Essential Creativity – The Birthday Song.*

MOTIVATION

Allow students to determine which instrument section should enter first, second, etc in #141, *Tallis Canon Round*. Students then perform #141 in their arrangement.

ASSESSMENT OF OBJECTIVES

1. Ask students to perform #140, *Bingo* and observe if they are using the correct finger patterns for violin/viola or correct fingerings for cello/bass.

2. Ask students to describe how the musical form of a round like *Row, Row, Row Your Boat,* is different from a Theme and Variations musical form.

3. Ask students to sing and then play *The Birthday Song* using a two-eighth note rhythm pickup.

CLOSURE

- Summarize new concepts.

- Remind students to listen carefully to their F-natural/F♯ and C-natural/C♯ when they are practicing.

- Assign practice material based upon class performance.

UNIT 5   LESSON FIVE

OBJECTIVES	NATIONAL STANDARDS
At the end of instruction students should be able to:	
1. Play the pitches F, E, and D on the C string for viola, cello.	2
2. Play the lower octave C Major scale for viola, cello.	2

WARM-UP/REVIEW

• Upper octave C Major scale that incorporates the low-second finger on the A and D strings for violin and viola

• Second position for bass

STRATEGIES FOR TEACHING OBJECTIVES

1a. While viola and cello students are learning how to play on the C string, ask violins and basses to complete the special exercise written for them at the top of pg. 36.

1b. Demonstrate playing on the C string and point out to students how slowly you must pull the bow to produce a good tone. Students must understand that they must pull their bow much slower on the C string than on higher pitched strings.

1c. Demonstrate the pitches F, E, and D on the C string and ask students to find and play them on their instruments.

1d. Lead the students through the *Listening Skill* exercises that appear in the TM pg. 196. Carefully check viola and cello fingering and intonation.

1e. Practice #144, *Let's Read "C,"* #145, *Let's Read "F,"* #146, *Let's Read "E,"* and #147, *Let's Read "D"* with all instruments. Students should master each exercise before proceeding to the next one. Remind students that there are no sharps or flats in the C Major scale.

1f. Ask students to read aloud the names of the notes in exercise #148, *Side By Side* before playing it.

2a. Ask students to pizzicato #149 and say or sing the note names.

2b. Ask viola and cello students to play #149 arco, while violin and bass students play pizzicato.

2c. Ask all students to play #149 arco.

MOTIVATION

Ask students to play #149, *C Major Scale* with slurs or different bow strokes (detaché, staccato or hooked bowing.). Teacher may wish to model some of these variations first.

ASSESSMENT OF OBJECTIVES

1. Ask students to play #149, *C Major Scale,* checking intonation, fingering, sound production and slower bow speed on the C string.

2. Ask viola and cello students to play a two-octave C Major scale beginning on the open C string.

CLOSURE

- Summarize new concepts.

- Remind viola students to move their left elbow more toward the center of the body when playing on the C string.

- Assign practice material based upon class performance.

UNIT 5 LESSON SIX

OBJECTIVES	NATIONAL STANDARDS
At the end of instruction students should be able to:	
1. Define and count a whole note and whole rest.	5
2. Define arpeggio.	5
3. Play C, D, E and F-natural with increased proficiency on the C string for viola/cello.	2
4. Play fourth finger G on the C string for viola.	2

WARM-UP/REVIEW

• F, E and D pitches on the C string (viola/cello)

• C Major scale

• Toe tapping while counting

STRATEGIES FOR TEACHING OBJECTIVES

1a. Demonstrate how to count and play whole notes and whole rests.

1b. Ask students to practice drawing whole notes, whole rests and half rests.

1c. Demonstrate how slowly students should pull their bows during whole notes. Contrast this with the bow speed required for quarter and half notes. An effective strategy for teaching students to pull their bows slowly is a miles-per-hour analogy, i.e., bows travel 45 miles-per-hour for quarter notes, 30 miles-per-hour for half notes, and 15 miles-per-hour for whole notes.

1d. Rehearse #150, *Rhythm Rap* with students while counting out loud and bowing in the air. Use any rhythm counting system you prefer. Then rehearse #151, *Slow Bows*.

2. Read aloud the definition of arpeggio and demonstrate arpeggios in C Major, D Major and G Major.

3. Rehearse violas and cellos separately on #152, *Long, Long Ago* and #153, *C Major Scale And Arpeggio* to increase students' proficiency of playing on the C string. Point out to viola students that the fourth finger on the C string sounds G, the pitch of their open G string.

4a. Ask violas to play F♯ followed by fourth finger G on the C string. Then ask them to match their fourth finger G to their open G string. Play echo patterns for them that incorporate F-natural and fourth finger G on the C string to reinforce their fingering skills.

4b. Rehearse #152, *Long, Long Ago,* emphasizing and tuning the viola fourth finger G on the C string to the cello and bass open G string.

4c. Rehearse #154, *Listen To Our Sections,* and #155, *Monday's Melody.* Students should master each exercise before proceeding to the next one.

MOTIVATION

Select one student to play #152, *Long, Long Ago* from the beginning. The student may stop at any time and call on another student to continue playing the melody. That student may stop anywhere and choose someone else to continue playing the melody. Continue the process until the end of the melody.

ASSESSMENT OF OBJECTIVES

1. Ask students to alternate counting and playing #151, *Slow Bows*.

2. Ask students to define arpeggio and play the arpeggio in the last four bars of #153, *C Major Scale And Arpeggio*.

3. Ask violas and cellos to play the first eight measures of #155, *Monday's Melody* and evaluate their sound production on the C string, bow speed and intonation.

4. Ask violas to play the pitch pattern C, D, F-natural, fourth finger G, and evaluate their fourth finger G intonation.

CLOSURE

- Summarize new concepts.

- Remind students to carefully count when playing whole notes.

- Remind students to pull their bows slowly when playing whole notes.

- Assign practice material based upon class performance.

UNIT 5 LESSON SEVEN

OBJECTIVES	NATIONAL STANDARDS
At the end of instruction students should be able to:	
1. Play E, A, G and F♯ on the E string for violin.	2
2. Play fourth finger on A string for the pitch E for viola.	2
3. Play F♯ in first position on the E string for bass.	2

WARM-UP/REVIEW

- C Major scale

- Arpeggio

- Fourth finger on the A, D and G strings for violin/viola

- Whole note and whole rest

STRATEGIES FOR TEACHING OBJECTIVES

1a. While violins and basses are learning new notes, ask violas and cellos to complete the written exercises on student pg. 38.

1b. Choose a violin student to demonstrate the pitches A, G and F♯ on the E string and have the other students find and play them on their violins. Explain and demonstrate how fast and lightly the bow must travel on the E string to produce a desirable sound. Be careful that students use less weight on the bow while playing the E string as compared to the other strings. Also, a straight bow is essential for an acceptable sound.

1c. Play sample *Listening Skills* (TM pg. 207) for all students to echo.

1d. Practice #156, *Let's Read "E,"* #157, *Let's Read "A,"* #158, *Let's Read "G,"* and #159, *Let's Read "F,"* with all instruments for violins and basses to learn new notes. Students should master each exercise before proceeding to the next one.

2a. Ask violas to tune their fourth finger E on the A string while violins play their open E string.

2b. Ask violins to tune their third finger D on the A string to their open D string and then practice matching their fourth finger E to their open E string.

2c. Ask violins to tune their third finger A on the E string to their A string and practice playing the interval from A to B on the E string, making sure the B is a full whole step away from A.

2d. Ask students to practice #160, *Moving Along,* #161, *G Major Scale,* #162, *Shepherd's Hey,* and #163, *Big Rock Candy Mountain.*

3a. Basses demonstrate first finger F♯ on the E string. Demonstrate how slowly the bow must travel on the E string to produce a desirable sound. The bow must travel much slower on the E string than on any other bass string. Also be sure basses have enough rosin on their bow hair to help produce the best sound possible on the E string. Upper string rosin should not be used on bass bows, only rosin especially produced for bass bows.

3b. Ask basses to practice playing F♯ on the E string. Check to see that all of their fingers are poised over the string and that the thumb is behind their second finger.

MOTIVATION

Challenge students to find at least two Ds, two As and two F♯s on their instruments.

ASSESSMENT OF OBJECTIVES

1. Ask violins to play #160, *Moving Along* and evaluate their E string notes, sound production, left hand shape and intonation.

2. Ask violas to play #156, *Let's Read "E"* and evaluate their sound production, left hand shape and intonation.

3. Ask basses to play #156, *Let's Read "E"* and #159, *Let's Read "F♯"* and evaluate their E string sound production, left hand shape and intonation.

CLOSURE

- Summarize new concepts.

- Remind students to listen carefully and keep their left hand carefully shaped when practicing, especially when learning new notes on their instrument.

- Assign practice material based upon class performance.

UNIT 5 LESSON EIGHT

OBJECTIVES	NATIONAL STANDARDS
At the end of instruction students should be able to: 1. Play fourth finger B on the E string for violin.	2

WARM-UP/REVIEW

• E, F♯, G and A on the E string for violin

• Fourth finger E on the A string for violin/viola

• E and F♯ on the E string for bass

• 1st and 2nd endings

STRATEGIES FOR TEACHING OBJECTIVES

1a. Violins demonstrate how to play fourth finger B on the E string.

1b. Ask violins to tune their third finger A on the E string to their open A string and then practice playing the interval of A to B on the E string.

1c. Play *Listening Skills* (TM pg. 215) and ask students to echo.

1d. All students practice #164, *Let's Read "B"*.

1e. Ask students to listen carefully and adjust their intonation if necessary on the Bs in #165, *Ice Skating* and #166, *Essential Elements Quiz – Academic Festival Overture Theme*.

MOTIVATION

Challenge students to find and play three Bs on their instrument. They must play them in tune to meet the challenge!

ASSESSMENT OF OBJECTIVES

1. Ask students to play #166, *Essential Elements Quiz – Academic Festival Overture Theme* and evaluate their fourth finger B on the E string (violins) and tone production. A sample playing quiz is available on pg. 132 based on the objectives identified on TM pg. 217.

CLOSURE

- Summarize new concepts.

- Remind students that only by practicing carefully will they learn to play their instruments well.

- Assign practice material based upon class performance.

UNIT 6 LESSON ONE

OBJECTIVES	NATIONAL STANDARDS
At the end of instruction students should be able to:	
1. Define staccato.	5
2. Demonstrate staccato bowing.	2
3. Play a G Major scale, including the upper octave and 4th finger on the A string for violin.	2

WARM-UP/REVIEW

• Parallel bowing

• F-natural and F♯

• C-natural and C♯

• G Major scale

STRATEGIES FOR TEACHING OBJECTIVES

1. Read aloud the definition of staccato. Ask students to identify the staccato pitches in #167, *Play Staccato.*

2a. Demonstrate staccato bowing on the open D string. Show students how to slightly pinch the bow stick with their index finger to start each staccato stroke. Show students how to stop the stroke by stopping their bow arm and slightly pinching the bow stick at the same time.

2b. Ask students to practice staccato bowing on open D strings. Have them say "KA" and imitate the sound at the beginning of their staccato stroke.

2c. Ask students to play the D Major scale with staccato bowing.

2d. Ask students to play #167, *Play Staccato.*

2e. Rehearse #168, *Arkansas Traveler.*

3a. Rehearse #169, *Skill Builders.* Sustain and tune each pitch so that the violins may review the E string notes.

3b. Demonstrate for students the detaché eighth notes and the staccato quarter notes in #170. Then rehearse the students playing the exercise.

3c. Reinforce the three-note slurs in #171. Be sure students change their bows together, carefully following the slurs.

3d. Rehearse #172–173.

MOTIVATION

Play simple *Listening Skills* echo patterns that incorporate staccato and G Major scale notes.

ASSESSMENT OF OBJECTIVES

1. Ask students to explain the difference between staccato and detaché bowing.

2. Ask students to play #168, *Arkansas Traveler* and evaluate staccato bowing.

3. Ask students to perform a G Major scale. Violins should play the upper octave while the remainder of the class repeats the lower octave. Aurally assess the mastery of the pitches for violins.

CLOSURE

- Summarize new concepts.

- Remind students to listen carefully to keep Cs in tune when they are practicing.

- Assign practice material based upon class performance.

UNIT 6 LESSON TWO

OBJECTIVES	NATIONAL STANDARDS
At the end of instruction students should be able to:	
1. Define hooked bowing.	5
2. Demonstrate hooked bowing.	2
3. Play the C Major scale, including the lower octave on the C string for viola and cello.	2

WARM-UP/REVIEW

• E string notes on the violin

• G Major scale, including E string notes on the violin

• Staccato bowing

STRATEGIES FOR TEACHING OBJECTIVES

1. Read aloud the definition of hooked bowing.

2a. Ask students to bow #174, *Hooked On D Major* in the air with hooked bow motions.

2b. Ask part of the class to play pizzicato while the remaining students play with hooked bowing. The hooked staccato notes should sound like pizzicatos. Be sure there is a definite stop between the hooked notes and that bows are moving in the same direction.

2c. Practice hooked bowing on open strings and then on familiar scales.

2d. Rehearse #175 and #176, emphasizing hooked bowing.

3a. Sustain and tune each pitch of #177 and then play with the rhythm as written.

3b. Rehearse #178–180. Point out to students the hooked bowing in exercise #180 and how it contrasts with the legato slurs.

MOTIVATION

Play simple *Listening Skills* echo patterns that incorporate staccato and hooked bowing.

ASSESSMENT OF OBJECTIVES

1. Ask students to explain the difference between staccato bowing and hooked bowing.

2. Ask students to play a D Major scale with two-note hooked bowing.

3. Ask students to play a C Major scale, including the lower octave on the C string on viola and cello. Evaluate the intonation and fingering of each student's performance.

CLOSURE

• Summarize new concepts.

• Remind students to completely stop their bow between staccato notes.

• Assign practice material based upon class performance.

UNIT 6 LESSON THREE

OBJECTIVES	NATIONAL STANDARDS
At the end of instruction students should be able to:	
1. Demonstrate forte and piano dynamics.	2
2. Play the D, C, and G Major scales and arpeggios, including the lower octave for viola and cello and the upper octave for violin.	2

WARM-UP/REVIEW

• E string notes on the violin

• G Major scale, including E string notes on the violin

• C Major scale, including C string notes for viola and cello

• Staccato and hooked bowing

STRATEGIES FOR TEACHING OBJECTIVES

1a. Ask students to play their open strings forte and piano. Demonstrate for students that they may add more weight to their bow, pull their bow faster and/or move it closer to the bridge to play louder. Ask students to experiment with each of these sound production variables.

1b. Rehearse #181, *Forte and Piano* and #182, *Surprise Symphony Theme*. Students should master each exercise, especially dynamics, before proceeding to the next one.

1c. Play a recorded example of the second movement of Haydn's *Symphony No. 94* and ask students to identify the surprise.

2a. Sustain and tune each pitch in the D, C, and G Major scales that appears in #183–187, *Skill Builders*. Review fingerings and the strings the students should use to play the scales properly.

2b. Ask students to play C, G and D scales at different dynamic levels.

2c. Ask students to practice writing "f" for forte and "p" for piano in their music.

2d. Have students select a familiar song they have learned and play it with forte and piano dynamics.

MOTIVATION

Select students to play their favorite melody as a solo while adding forte and piano dynamics.

ASSESSMENT OF OBJECTIVES

1. Ask students to play #182, *Surprise Symphony Theme* and evaluate staccato bowing and dynamics.

2. Ask students to play the D, C, and G Major scales in #182–187. Evaluate the intonation and fingering of the students' performance.

CLOSURE

- Summarize new concepts.

- Remind students to completely stop their bow between staccato notes.

- Assign practice material based upon class performance.

UNIT 6 LESSON FOUR

OBJECTIVES	NATIONAL STANDARDS
At the end of instruction students should be able to:	
1. Play orchestra arrangements on student book pgs. 43–45.	2
2. Define opera and opera overture.	6

WARM-UP/REVIEW

• E string notes on the violin

• G Major scale, including E string notes on the violin

• C Major scale, including both octaves for the viola and cello

• Forte and piano dynamics

• Measure numbers

• First and second endings

• D. C. al Fine

STRATEGIES FOR TEACHING OBJECTIVES

1a. Rehearse #188–192, *Performance Spotlight* orchestra arrangements. Explain to students how the A and B parts for each instrument section are divided. Try various combinations of A and B parts, allowing each instrument section an opportunity to play the melody.

1b. Discuss and teach the concept of balance so that the melody may always be heard over the accompaniment.

1c. Point out to students all the different dynamic markings that occur throughout the arrangements.

2. Define opera as a story that is sung. Play excerpts of famous operas and describe the story and plot of each. Explain that operas begin with an orchestral introduction known as an overture that includes the principal melodies of the work. Point out that Gioachini Rossini, composer of #190, *William Tell Overture* is one of the most famous opera composers in history.

MOTIVATION

Give students the opportunity to select which instrument sections play the A and B parts of the orchestral arrangements.

ASSESSMENT OF OBJECTIVES

1. Record the students' performances of the orchestral arrangements. Play the recording for the students and ask them to evaluate their performance. Give them specific criteria to listen for and discuss, such as balance, intonation, tone production, rhythm, and articulation.

2. Ask students to define the terms opera and opera overture.

CLOSURE

- Summarize new concepts.

- Remind students to completely stop their bow between staccato notes.

- Assign practice material based upon class performance.

UNIT 6 LESSON FIVE

OBJECTIVES	NATIONAL STANDARDS
At the end of instruction students should be able to:	
1. Define the term solo.	5
2. Perform a solo.	2

WARM-UP/REVIEW

• Hooked bowing

• Forte and piano

• D, G, and C Major scales

STRATEGIES FOR TEACHING OBJECTIVES

1a. Define the term solo. Show and play excerpts, either live or recorded, for each of the four string instruments.

1b. Describe how the piano is used to accompany a solo, and how it can provide the harmony, and even sometimes the melody, when a solo is played with keyboard accompaniment.

2a. Using the CD, play the recordings of the student solos, #193. Ask students to frequently play the CD at home as they learn to play the solo. Students should imitate the tone quality, intonation, style, and rhythm as demonstrated on the CD when they are practicing the solo.

2b. Give students the opportunity to select different tempi and dynamics in their solos. Ask them to evaluate what they have selected.

MOTIVATION

Play an excerpt of the solo for each string instrument. Deliberately play incorrect notes occasionally and ask the students to identify which notes are incorrect.

ASSESSMENT OF OBJECTIVES

1. Ask students to explain the difference between solo and orchestra music.

2. Ask students to play their solo. Evaluate dynamics, tone production, tempo, rhythm, and style.

CLOSURE

- Summarize new concepts.

- Assign practice material based upon class performance.

UNIT 6   LESSON SIX

OBJECTIVES	NATIONAL STANDARDS
At the end of instruction students should be able to:	
1. Improvise using rhythmic variation.	3
2. Improvise within the key of D Major.	3

WARM-UP/REVIEW

• Bowing quarter, half, and eighth notes

• Different rhythms in 4/4 meter using quarter, half, and eighth notes

STRATEGIES FOR TEACHING OBJECTIVES

1a. Ask students to tap their toes to a steady beat while making up rhythms on D Major scale pitches.

1b. Give students the opportunity to make up their own rhythm for each pitch of the D Major scale. Specify that the rhythms must comprise a full measure in 4/4 meter and only one pitch should be used per measure.

2a. Explain a pentatonic scale and demonstrate the D pentatonic scale. Give students the opportunity to practice it.

2b. Ask students to make up their own melody using only the pitches of the D pentatonic scale. To help students with their first attempts, specify the rhythms and note values the students may use while playing #194, *Rhythm Jam*.

2d. Give students the opportunity to play their melodies for each other using only the pitches of the D pentatonic scale.

2c. Select an instrument section to play their improvised melodies while accompanied by the rest of the orchestra playing the B part in exercise #195, *Instant Melody*.

2d. Select individual students or ask for individual student volunteers to play their improvised melody as a solo, accompanied by the rest of the orchestra playing the B part in exercise #195, *Instant Melody*.

MOTIVATION

Ask students to change the rhythm of a familiar melody such as *Twinkle, Twinkle Little Star* and play it for the class.

ASSESSMENT OF OBJECTIVES

1. Ask individual students to play rhythmic variations of a familiar melody.

2. Ask students to play an improvised solo using only the pitches of the D pentatonic scale. Students may freely choose their own notes, rhythms, style, and dynamics.

CLOSURE

- Summarize new concepts.

- Assign practice material based upon class performance.

THEORY

USING THE THEORY WORKSHEETS • QUIZZES

The following pages have been designed to help reinforce the knowledge needed to play a musical instrument. All students benefit from a variety of learning styles and some are more dependent upon one than another. Therefore, it is important to incorporate written work into the orchestra classroom at regular intervals.

These pages may be photocopied or printed from the PDF files, which will allow you to present them at your own pace and in whatever format you feel is most beneficial for each individual class. One option is to use them as worksheets to help reinforce concepts presented in the method achievement. Each page is correlated with a specific page number in the book. Also, at the completion of each book there is a "Music Fundamentals Final" which includes material from the entire book.

You are encouraged to use the pages consistently throughout the year in whatever format you choose. A few suggested ideas for incorporating them into the classroom are:

1. Have the entire class complete them together.

2. Rehearse certain instrument sections on the music, while the others do written work.

3. Have the entire class complete them as you have individuals perform playing quizzes.

4. Assign them as homework.

5. Leave them as assignments for the non-music substitute teacher when you are absent.

WORKSHEET • QUIZ
Unit 1
(may be used after student book page 5)

Activity

NAME _____

DATE _____

1. Name the four open strings on your instrument from the lowest to the highest.

2. *Pizzicato* means to _____ the string.

3. The _____ is the pulse of music.

4. The music staff has _____ lines and _____ spaces.

5. The top number in a time signature tells us how many _____ are in a measure.

6. The bottom number of a time signature tells us what kind of note gets _____ beat.

7. A _____ bar indicates the end of a piece of music.

8. Bar lines divide the music staff into _____ .

9. A quarter note gets _____ beat(s) of sound.

10. A quarter rest gets _____ beat(s) of silence.

11. A _____ sign indicates a new line of music and a set of note names.

12. The instrument I play is written in _____ clef.

Reproducible

WORSHEET • QUIZ
Unit 2

(may be used after student book page 15)

NAME _____

DATE _____

1. Match the following symbols to their definition:

   ___ ⊓   A. Up bow

   ___ :|| B. Sharp

   ___ V   C. Repeat sign

   ___ ♯   D. Down bow

2. *Dreidel* is an _____ folk song.

3. A _____ is a sequence of notes in ascending or descending order.

4. A _____ signature tells us what notes to play with sharps or flats throughout the entire piece.

5. Describe proper left hand position:

6. Name two pencil hold exercises:

RHYTHM & NOTE READING WORKSHEET • QUIZ
Unit 3

(may be used after student book page 15)

NAME _____

DATE _____

1. Draw the barlines in the proper place in the following line of music.

2. Complete each measure by adding the correct number of quarter notes or rests.

3. Write the letter names of the notes below the staff for your instrument only.
   Write the finger number you would use to play each note above it.

Violin

Viola

Cello & Bass

WORKSHEET • QUIZ
Unit 3

(may be used after student book page 21)

NAME _____

DATE _____

1. Define the following terms.

   A. Andante _____

   B. Moderato _____

   C. Allegro _____

   D. Arco _____

2. List four steps of practicing for success.

   _____

   _____

   _____

   _____

3. When playing a piece with a 1st and 2nd ending, you play the 1st ending

   _____ time(s).

4. When playing a piece with a 1st and 2nd ending, you play the 2nd ending

   _____ time(s).

5. A ⸖ means to _____ the bow and return to its starting point.

6. In $\frac{2}{4}$ time there are _____ beats per measure and the _____ note
   (or rest) gets one beat.

7. Two eighth notes equal _____ quarter note(s).

RHYTHM & NOTE READING WORKSHEET • QUIZ
Unit 3

(may be used after student book page 21)

Activity

NAME _____

DATE _____

1. Write the counts under the following rhythms:

2. Write the total number of beats in the blank.

3. Write the letter names of the notes below the staff for your instrument only.
   Write the finger number you would use to play each note above it.

Violin

Viola

Cello & Bass

Reproducible

107

WORKSHEET • QUIZ
Unit 4

(may be used after student book page 27)

NAME _____

DATE _____

1. ♩ = _____ beat(s) of sound.

2. ━ = _____ beat(s) of sound.

3. 4+ means to pluck the string with the fourth finger of the _____ hand.

4. ‖: :‖ means to _____ the section of music enclosed between the signs.

5. In the key of _____ Major, there is only one sharp (F♯) in the key signature.

6. In the key of _____ Major, there are two sharps (F♯ and C♯) in the key signature.

7. A great German composer named _____ wrote music even after he was completely deaf.

8. Common time (𝐜) is the same as _____ time.

9. Two or more pitches sounding at the same time is a _____ .

10. Name two important things that good performers must remember to do:

RHYTHM & NOTE READING WORKSHEET • QUIZ
Unit 4

(may be used after student book page 27)

Activity

NAME _____

DATE _____

1. Write the counts under the following rhythms:

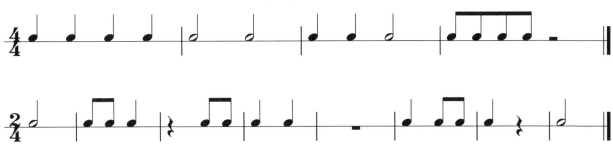

2. Complete each measure by adding the correct number of quarter notes or rests.

3. Write the letter names of the notes below the staff for your instrument only.
   Write the finger number you would use to play each note above it.

Violin

Viola

Cello & Bass

Reproducible

WORKSHEET • QUIZ
Unit 5
(may be used after student book page 31)

NAME _____

DATE _____

1. Fill in the total number of beats each of the following will receive:

    ♩ = _____ beat(s)   𝅘𝅥. = _____ beat(s)

    𝅗𝅥 = _____ beat(s)   ♩‿𝅗𝅥 = _____ beat(s)

    ♩‿♩ = _____ beat(s)   ♫ ♩ = _____ beat(s)

2. A dot after a note always adds _____ the value of the note.

3. In $\frac{3}{4}$ time there are _____ beats per measure and the _____ note (or rest) gets one beat.

4. Identify the following by writing "T" if it is a tie or "S" if it it a slur.

_____   _____   _____   _____   _____   _____

5. A note that comes before the first full measure is called an _____ .

6. The Italian term *Da Capo (D.C.)* means to return to the _____ .

7. The Italian term *Fine* means _____ .

RHYTHM & NOTE READING WORKSHEET • QUIZ
Unit 5

(may be used after student book page 31)

Activity

NAME _____

DATE _____

1. Write the counts under the following rhythms:

2. Write the letter names of the notes below the staff for your instrument only.
   Write the finger number you would use to play each note above it.

Violin

Viola

Cello & Bass

Reproducible

WORSHEET • QUIZ
Unit 6

(may be used after student book page 42)

NAME _____

DATE _____

1. A _____ sign cancels a sharp or flat.

2. A _____ step is the smallest distance between two notes.

3. Two half steps equal one _____ step.

4. A composition with two different parts played together is called a _____ .

5. Staccato notes are marked with a _____ above or below the note.

6. _____ bowing is two or more notes played in the same direction with a stop between each note.

7. A whole note gets _____ beat(s) of sound.

8. The key signature for C Major has _____ sharps and flats.

9. Forte means to play _____ .

10. Piano means to play _____ .

11. Write "H" if the distance between the following notes is a half step or "W" if the distance is a whole step:

_____ D–E

_____ F♯–G

_____ E–F

_____ F–G

_____ G–A

_____ C♯–D

RHYTHM & NOTE READING WORKSHEET • QUIZ
Unit 6

(may be used after student book page 42)

Activity

NAME _____

DATE _____

1. Write the counts under the following rhythms:

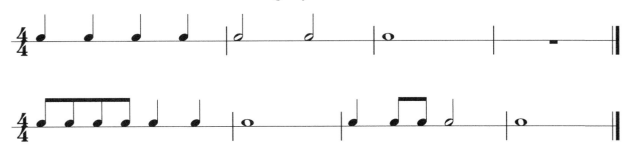

2. Write the letter names of the notes below the staff for your instrument only.
   Write the finger number you would use to play each note above it.

Violin

Viola

Cello

Bass

Reproducible

Listening

LISTENING FOR DYNAMICS

(any lesson)

NAME _____

DATE _____

Dynamic contrasts (changes in loud and soft) are one of the most important ways to make music interesting and expressive. As you develop your musicianship, you will become more aware of dynamic changes.

Listen to the three examples. Decide which description best depicts what you hear.

1. _____   A. [soft] **LOUD** [soft] **LOUD**

2. _____   B. **LOUD** [soft] **LOUD** [soft] **LOUD**

3. _____   C. **LOUD**

D. No changes in dynamic level

Reproducible

LISTENING FOR METER

(any lesson after student page 28)

CD-ROM Tracks 4–7

Listening

NAME _____

DATE _____

The meter of a piece of music is determined by the time signature, like $\frac{4}{4}$ or $\frac{3}{4}$. In $\frac{4}{4}$ meter there are four beats per measure and the pulse can be felt in sets of four (1–2, 3–4). In $\frac{3}{4}$ meter there are three beats per measure and the pulse can be felt in sets of three (1–2–3, 1–2–3). Listen to the following examples and determine whether the music is written in $\frac{4}{4}$ meter or $\frac{3}{4}$ meter. Circle the correct answer.

1. $\frac{4}{4}$ $\frac{3}{4}$

2. $\frac{4}{4}$ $\frac{3}{4}$

3. $\frac{4}{4}$ $\frac{3}{4}$

4. $\frac{4}{4}$ $\frac{3}{4}$

Reproducible

MUSIC FUNDAMENTALS FINAL

NAME _____

DATE _____

1. Identify the following key signatures:

    Two sharps: _____ Major

    No sharps or flats: _____ Major

    One sharp: _____ Major

2. Write the counts under the following rhythms:

3. Match the following terms to their definition:

_____ Allegro	A. Smallest distance between 2 notes
_____ Forte	B. Play loudly
_____ Harmony	C. Pluck the strings
_____ Pizzicato	D. Move bow away from body
_____ Beat	E. Slow walking tempo
_____ Half step	F. Two or more different pitches sounding at the same time
_____ Andante	G. Play softly
_____ Double bar	H. Moderate tempo
_____ Up bow	I. Indicates the end of a piece of music
_____ Moderato	J. Fast bright tempo
_____ Piano	K. Move bow toward body
_____ Down bow	L. The pulse of music

NAME _____ Activity

DATE _____

4. Write the letter names of the notes below the staff for your instrument only.

Violin

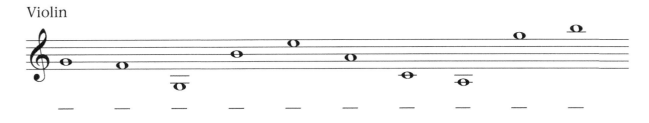

Viola

Cello

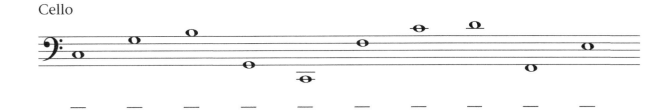

Bass

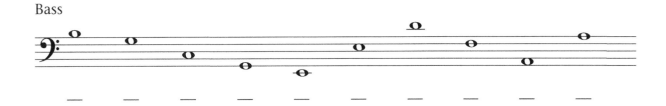

Reproducible

PERFORMANCE

YOUR INSTRUMENT

How did you choose the instrument you play in orchestra? Why? Write a short essay about your instrument. Include information about the history of your instrument, why and how you chose it, and what you enjoy most about playing music. You may find historical information on page 1 of your book, and you may also wish to include additional information from other sources. On the back page of your essay draw or trace a picture of your instrument (page 2 of your book) and label the parts. Plan to share your essay with the class.

#9. ESSENTIAL ELEMENTS QUIZ
(Unit 1, Lesson Three)

Assessment

NAME _____

DATE _____

SKILL	POSSIBLE POINTS	SCORE
Posture & Playing Position	25	
Pizzicato Correct String	25	
Counting Quarter Notes/Rests	25	
Steady Beat	15	
Say/Sing Note Names	10	

TOTAL _____

GRADE _____

Reproducible

121

#16. ESSENTIAL ELEMENTS QUIZ
(Unit 2, Lesson One)

Assessment

NAME _____

DATE _____

SKILL	POSSIBLE POINTS	SCORE
Posture & Playing Position	20	
Left Hand Shape (Square first finger for violin and viola)	20	
Pizzicato Correct String	15	
Counting Quarter Notes/Rests	15	
Steady Beat	15	
Drawing Correct Symbols	15	

TOTAL _____

GRADE _____

#22. ESSENTIAL ELEMENTS QUIZ – LIGHTLY ROW
(Unit 2, Lesson Three)

Assessment

NAME _____

DATE _____

SKILL	POSSIBLE POINTS	SCORE
Posture & Playing Position (Shoulder Position for violin and viola)	20	
Left Hand Shape	20	
Pizzicato Correct Notes	20	
Keeping Fingers Down (for violin, viola, and cello)	10	
Counting Quarter Notes/Rests	10	
Steady Beat	10	
Say/Sing Note Names	10	

TOTAL _____

GRADE _____

Reproducible

#32. ESSENTIAL ELEMENTS QUIZ –
UP THE D SCALE
(Unit 2, Lesson Five)

NAME _____

DATE _____

SKILL	POSSIBLE POINTS	SCORE
Posture & Playing Position	20	
Left Hand Shape	20	
Pizzicato Correct Notes (Shifting for basses)	20	
Counting Quarter Notes/Rests	15	
Steady Beat	15	
Say/Sing Note Names	10	

TOTAL _____

GRADE _____

#53. ESSENTIAL ELEMENTS QUIZ – OLYMPIC CHALLENGE

(Unit 3, Lesson Two)

Assessment

NAME _____

DATE _____

SKILL	POSSIBLE POINTS	SCORE
Posture & Playing Position	20	
Bow Hand Shape	20	
Correct Arm Movement for String Level	20	
Rhythm	10	
Parallel Bowing	15	
Tone	15	

TOTAL _____

GRADE _____

Reproducible

125

#64. ESSENTIAL ELEMENTS QUIZ – THE D MAJOR SCALE

(Unit 3, Lesson Four)

Assessment

NAME _____

DATE _____

SKILL	POSSIBLE POINTS	SCORE
Posture & Playing Position	20	
Bow Hand Shape	20	
Left Hand Shape	20	
Parallel Bowing	10	
Steady Beat	10	
Half Steps and Whole Steps	10	
Tone Quality	10	

TOTAL _____

GRADE _____

Reproducible

#76. ESSENTIAL ELEMENTS QUIZ – FOR PETE'S SAKE

(Unit 3, Lesson Six)

Assessment

NAME _____

DATE _____

SKILL	POSSIBLE POINTS	SCORE
Posture & Playing Position	15	
Bowing	15	
Left Hand Shape	15	
Intonation	10	
Repeats/1st and 2nd Endings	15	
Correct Notes	10	
Counting Eighth Notes	20	

TOTAL _____

GRADE _____

Reproducible

#86. ESSENTIAL ELEMENTS QUIZ –
ODE TO JOY

(Unit 3, Lesson Eight)

NAME _____

DATE _____

SKILL	POSSIBLE POINTS	SCORE
Posture & Playing Position	15	
Bow Hand Shape	15	
Left Hand Shape	15	
Intonation	20	
Rhythm	15	
Correct Fingerings (4th finger upper strings)	20	

TOTAL _____

GRADE _____

#102. ESSENTIAL ELEMENTS QUIZ –
THIS OLD MAN
(Unit 4, Lesson Four)

Assessment

NAME _____

DATE _____

SKILL	POSSIBLE POINTS	SCORE
Posture & Playing Position	20	
Bow Hand Shape	15	
Left Hand Shape	15	
Intonation	10	
Correct Rhythm	10	
Correct G String Pitches	20	
Tone Quality	10	

TOTAL _____

GRADE _____

Reproducible

#107. ESSENTIAL ELEMENTS QUIZ – SAILOR'S SONG
(Unit 4, Lesson Five)

NAME _____

DATE _____

SKILL	POSSIBLE POINTS	SCORE
Posture & Playing Position	15	
Bow Hand Shape and Parallel Bowing	15	
Correct Notes	10	
Intonation	15	
Writing in Correct Time Signature	10	
Correct 3/4 Rhythm	20	
Tone Quality	15	

TOTAL _____

GRADE _____

#139. ESSENTIAL ELEMENTS QUIZ – RUSSIAN FOLK TUNE
(Unit 5, Lesson Three)

Assessment

NAME _____

DATE _____

SKILL	POSSIBLE POINTS	SCORE
Posture & Playing Position	5	
Correct Notes	10	
Rhythm	5	
Bow Hand Shape and Parallel Bowing	10	
Slurring	20	
F♮ and C♮ Fingering and Intonation	20	
General Intonation	20	
Tone Quality	10	

TOTAL _____

GRADE _____

Reproducible

#166. ESSENTIAL ELEMENTS QUIZ – ACADEMIC FESTIVAL THEME
(Unit 5, Lesson Eight)

NAME _____

DATE _____

SKILL	POSSIBLE POINTS	SCORE
Posture & Playing Position	10	
Correct Notes (E string violin)	25	
Rhythm	15	
Bow Hand Shape and Parallel Bowing	10	
Tone Quality	20	
General Intonation	20	

TOTAL _____

GRADE _____

PARTICIPANT CONCERT ETIQUETTE

NAME _____

DATE _____

When you attend a concert, ballet, opera, or theater production, there are certain audience behavior expectations. But as a member of a performing group, there are also participant behavior expectations. When you are on the concert stage, many people are watching how you perform and present yourself.

Let's look at some basic participant behavior guidelines that are appropriate for formal musical concerts.

- Plan to arrive in plenty of time to assemble your instrument, warm-up, and gather your music. Check that your music stand and all other equipment is in place.

- In advance, make sure that your instrument is in top working condition. Make sure you have a shoulder pad or rock stop, along with a good cake of rosin. It is also a good idea to have extra strings in your case.

- If there is a dress code or uniform, it is very important that you observe it. Being a member of the orchestra is being a member of a team. All must conform to present the orchestra in the best possible way.

- During the concert, you must focus all your attention on the director. Avoid looking at the audience. You must watch the director closely for all starting and stopping cues.

- It is inappropriate to eat, drink or chew gum during a concert.

- Maintain good posture and a positive stage presence at all times when on stage. You are representing not only yourself, but the entire orchestra as well.

- Play with your very best effort. One purpose of the concert is to show others how hard you have worked to prepare for this event. Enjoy making beautiful music!

List three appropriate behaviors you feel are most important to remember when performing a formal concert.

a)

b)

c)

AUDIENCE CONCERT ETIQUETTE

NAME _____

DATE _____

Whether you are attending the opera, the ballet, a theater production, a marching band half time show, a rock concert, or a formal musical concert, specific guidelines dictate appropriate behavior for each particular event. Understanding the common courtesies involved for each different event allows everyone involved, including both performer and the audience, to enjoy the performance.

Let's look at some basic audience behavior guidelines that are appropriate for formal musical concerts.

• Plan to arrive on time. If you do arrive after the performance has begun, wait outside the auditorium until a break between selections (the audience is clapping) to enter the concert hall.

• Talking or rustling around during a performance keeps others in the audience from both hearing and enjoying the concert. The behavior may also distract the performers.

• Cellular telephones should remain off during any performance. If you must wear a beeper, make sure it is set so no audible sound will be heard.

• When young children attend a formal concert, they learn to be good audience participants. Crying, chattering and otherwise noisy children, however, should be removed from a performance immediately and should return only if such behavior does not continue.

• Catcalls, whistling, or other loud audible noises are best reserved for athletic events or other similar activities, and are never appropriate at formal concerts.

List three appropriate behaviors you feel are most important to remember when attending a formal concert.

a)

b)

c)

Reproducible

STUDENT SELF ASSESSMENT
CONCERT PERFORMANCE

Assessment

NAME _____

DATE OF CONCERT_____

1. List 3 things you learned in preparing and presenting your performance:

    a.

    b.

    c.

2. List 3 things you did well during the performance:

    a.

    b.

    c.

3. List 3 things you could have done better during the performance:

    a.

    b.

    c.

4. Name your favorite piece played on the concert:

    Why?

5. Rate your overall performance at the concert on a scale 1-10 with 10 being the highest:

Reprodu

TEACHER ASSESSMENT – SOLO PERFORMANCE

STUDENT NAME _____ _____

DATE _____

Solo or Exercise:

1. Posture and playing position

2. Tone quality (characteristic tone)

3. Notes and accuracy (correct notes, key signature, accidentals)

4. Intonation

5. Rhythm and tempo

6. Bowing

7. Dynamics

8. Stage presence and musical presentation

9. Other comments

Grade _____

HISTORY

400 AD	600	800	1000	1200	1400

MUSIC

During the Middle Ages (also called the *Medieval Period*), the Roman Catholic church was the most powerful influence in European life. The church's music was a collection of ancient melodies called *plain-song* or *chant*, sung in unison (single line) with Latin words. The chants were organized in about 600 AD by Pope Gregory, and these official versions are known as *Gregorian chant*. Later, simple harmonies were added, and eventually the harmony parts became independent melodies sung with the main tune. This is called *polyphony*. Church music was written down using *neumes*, or square notes.

Outside the churches, traveling entertainers called *troubadours* or *minstrels* would sing songs about life and love in the language of the common people. This music was more lively and would often be accompanied by a drum, a wooden flute or an early form of the guitar called a *lute*.

- Plainsong
- Gregorian Chant
- Harmony
- Polyphony
- Troubadours

400 AD	600	800	1000	1200	1400

ART & LITERATURE

- Romanesque architecture
- Gothic architecture
- Dante, author *(The Divine Comedy)*
- Chaucer, author *(Canterbury Tales)*
- Donatello, artist *(David)*

400 AD	600	800	1000	1200	1400

WORLD EVENTS

- Fall of Roman Empire *(476 AD)*
- Charlemagne, Holy Roman Emperor
- First Crusade begins *(1096)*
- The Black Death *(bubonic plague)*
- Rise of European universities
- Muhammad, prophet of Islam faith
- The Magna Carta *(1215)*
- Hindu-Arabic numbers developed
- Gunpowder, compass, paper invented *(China)*
- Genghis Kahn rules Asia
- Marco Polo travels to China
- Mayan civilization
- Incan and Aztec civilizations

THE RENAISSANCE

| 1450 | 1500 | 1550 | 1600 |

MUSIC

The era from about 1450–1600 was called the *Renaissance* ("rebirth") because people wanted to recreate the artistic and scientific glories of ancient Greece and Rome. It was also a time of discovery. The new printing press brought music to the homes of the growing middle class. European society became more *secular*, or non-religious, and concerts were featured in the halls of the nobility. An entertaining form of secular songs was the *madrigal*, sung by 4 or 5 voices at many special occasions. Instrumental music became popular, as new string, brass and woodwind instruments were developed.

A form of church music was the *motet*, with 3 or 4 independent vocal parts. In the new Protestant churches, the entire congregation sang *chorales*: simple melodies in even rhythms like the hymns we hear today. Important Renaissance composers were Josquin des Pres, Palestrina, Gabrielli, Monteverdi, William Byrd and Thomas Tallis (*Tallis Canon**).

• Protestant church music

• First printed music   • Madrigals

*music featured in Book 1

| 1450 | 1500 | 1550 | 1600 |

ART & LITERATURE

• Leonardo da Vinci, scientist/artist
(*Mona Lisa, The Last Supper*)

   • Michelangelo, artist
   (*Sistine Chapel, David*)

      • Machiavelli,
      author (*The Prince*)

• Shakespeare, author
(*Romeo and Juliet, Hamlet*)

| 1450 | 1500 | 1550 | 1600 |

WORLD EVENTS

• Gutenberg invents printing press *(1454)*   • Martin Luther ignites Protestant Reformation *(1517)*

   • Columbus travels to America *(1492)*

      • Magellan circles globe *(1519)*

         • Copernicus begins modern astronomy *(1543)*

         • First European contact with Japan *(1549)*

139

Reproducible

| 1600 | 1650 | 1700 | 1750 |

MUSIC

Music and the arts (and even clothing) became fancier and more dramatic in the *Baroque* era (about 1600–1750). Like the fancy decorations of Baroque church architecture, melodies were often played with *grace notes*, or quick nearby tones added to decorate them. Rhythms became more complex with time signatures, bar lines and faster-moving melodic lines. Our now familiar major and minor scales formed the basis for harmony, and chords were standardized to what we often hear today.

The harpsichord became the most popular keyboard instrument, with players often *improvising* (making up) their parts using the composer's chords and bass line. Violin making reached new heights in Italy. Operas, ballets and small orchestras were beginning to take shape, as composers specified the exact instruments, tempos and dynamics to be performed.

- Henry Purcell *(1659–1695), Rigaudon*, Trumpet Tune*
  - Antonio Vivaldi *(1676–1741), The Four Seasons*
    - Jean Joseph Mouret *(1682–1738), Rondeau**
      - George Frideric Handel *(1685–1759), Messiah*
        - Johann Sebastian Bach *(1685–1750), Minuet*, Musette*, Peasant's Cantata**

- First public opera house *(Vienna, 1637)*
- Stradivarius violins *(1700–1737)*
  - First piano built *(1709)*

*music featured in Books 1 & 2

| 1600 | 1650 | 1700 | 1750 |

ART & LITERATURE

- Cervantes, author *(Don Quixote)*
- Milton, author *(Paradise Lost)*
- Defoe, author *(Robinson Crusoe)*

- Rubens, artist *(Descent from the Cross)*
- Kabuki theater in Japan

- Rembrandt, artist *(The Night Watch)*
- Swift, author *(Gulliver's Travels)*

- Taj Mahal built *(1634–1653)*

| 1600 | 1650 | 1700 | 1750 |

WORLD EVENTS

- Salem witchcraft trials *(1692)*

- Galileo identifies gravity *(1602)*
- Louis XIV builds Versailles Palace *(1661–1708)*

- First English colony in America *(Jamestown, 1607)*

- Quebec founded by Champlain *(1608)*

- First slaves to America *(1619)*

- Isaac Newton *(1642-1727)* formulates principals of physics and math

Reproducible

THE CLASSICAL ERA

1750	1775	1800	1820

MUSIC

The *Classical* era, from about 1750 to the early 1800's, was a time of great contrasts. While patriots fought for the rights of the common people in the American and French revolutions, composers were employed to entertain wealthy nobles and aristocrats. Music became simpler and more elegant, with melodies often flowing over accompaniment patterns in regular 4-bar phrases. Like the architecture of ancient *Classical* Greece, music was fit together in "building blocks" by balancing one phrase against another, or one entire section against another.

The piano replaced the harpsichord and became the most popular instrument for the *concerto* (solo) with orchestra accompaniment. The string quartet became the favorite form of *chamber* (small group) music, and orchestra concerts featured *symphonies* (longer compositions with 4 contrasting parts or *movements*). Toward the end of this era, Beethoven's changing musical style led the way toward the more emotional and personal expression of Romantic music.

- Franz Josef Haydn *(1732–1809), Surprise Symphony*, Theme from London Symphony**
  - Wolfgang Amadeus Mozart *(1756–1791), A Mozart Melody**
    - Ludwig van Beethoven *(1770–1827), Ode To Joy*, Theme from Violin Concerto**

*music featured in Books 1 & 2

1750	1775	1800	1820

ART & LITERATURE

- Samuel Johnson, author *(Dictionary)*

  - Voltaire, author *(Candide)*

    - Gainsborough, artist *(The Blue Boy)*

    - *Encyclopedia Britannica*, first edition

- Wm. Wordsworth, author *(Lyrical Ballads)*

  - Goethe, author *(Faust)*

    - Goya, artist *(Witch's Sabbath)*

    - Jane Austen, author *(Pride and Prejudice)*

1750	1775	1800	1820

WORLD EVENTS

- Ben Franklin discovers electricity *(1751)*

  - American Revolution *(1775–1783)*

    - French Revolution *(1789–1794)*

      - Napoleon crowned Emperor of France *(1804)*

      - Lewis and Clark explore northwest *(1804)*

        - Metronome invented *(1815)*

          - First steamship crosses Atlantic *(1819)*

141

Reproducible

THE ROMANTIC ERA

1820	1840	1860	1880	1900

MUSIC

The last compositions of Beethoven were among the first of the new *Romantic* era, lasting from the early 1800's to about 1900. No longer employed by churches or nobles, composers became free from Classical restraints and expressed their personal emotions through their music. Instead of simple titles like *Concerto* or *Symphony*, they would often add descriptive titles like *Witches' Dance* or *To The New World*. Orchestras became larger, including nearly all the standard instruments we now use. Composers began to write much more difficult and complex music, featuring more "colorful" instrument combinations and harmonies.

Nationalism was an important trend in this era. Composers used folk music and folk legends (especially in Russia, eastern Europe and Scandinavia) to identify their music with their native lands. Today's concert audiences still generally prefer the drama of Romantic music to any other kind.

- Gioacchino Rossini *(1792–1868), William Tell Overture**
- Charles Gounod *(1818–1893), Theme from Faust*
- Jacques Offenbach *(1819–1880), Can Can***, Barcarolle**
  - Johannes Brahms *(1833–1897), Symphony No. 1*, Academic Festival Overture Theme*
    - P. I. Tchaikovsky *(1840–1893), Symphony No. 4, March from The Nutcracker*
      - Anton Dvorak *(1841–1904), Theme from New World Symphony**
- Gustav Mahler *(1860–1911), Mahler's Theme**
  - Edward MacDowell *(1861–1908), To A Wild Rose*
  - Edward Elgar *(1857–1934), Pomp And Circumstance**   • Gustav Holst *(1874–1934), In The Bleak Midwinter**

*music featured in Books 1 & 2

1820	1840	1860	1880	1900

ART & LITERATURE

- Charles Dickens, author *(The Pickwick Papers, David Copperfield)*

- Pierre Renoir, artist *(Luncheon of the Boating Party)*

- Harriet Beecher Stowe, author *(Uncle Tom's Cabin)*

- Lewis Carroll, author *(Alice In Wonderland)*

- Louisa May Alcott, author *(Little Women)*

- Jules Verne, author *(20,000 Leagues Under The Sea)*
  - Claude Monet, artist *(Gare Saint-Lazare)*
- Mark Twain, author *(Tom Sawyer, Huckleberry Finn)*

- Vincent van Gogh, artist *(The Sunflowers)*

- Rudyard Kipling, author *(Jungle Book)*

1820	1840	1860	1880	1900

WORLD EVENTS

- First railroad *(1830)*
  - Samuel Morse invents telegraph *(1837)*
  - First photography *(1838)*

- American Civil War *(1861–1865)*

- Alexander Graham Bell invents telephone *(1876)*

- Edison invents phonograph, practical light bulb, movie projector *(1877–1888)*

1900   **1925**   **1950**   **1975**   **2000**

MUSIC

The *20th century* was a diverse era of new ideas that "broke the rules" of traditional music. Styles of music moved in many different directions.

Impressionist composers Debussy and Ravel wrote music that seems more vague and blurred than the Romantics. New slightly-dis-sonant chords were used, and like Impressionist paintings, much of their music describes an impression of nature.

Composer Arnold Schoenberg devised a way to throw away all the old ideas of harmony by creating *12-tone* music. All 12 tones of the chromatic scale were used equally, with no single pitch forming a "key center."

Some of the music of Stravinsky and others was written in a *Neo-Classical* style (or "new" classical). This was a return to the Classical principals of balance and form, and to music that did *not* describe any scene or emotion.

Composers have experimented with many ideas: some music is based on the laws of chance, some is drawn on graph paper, some lets the performers decide when or what to play, and some is combined with electronic or other sounds.

Popular music like jazz, country, folk, and rock & roll has had a significant impact on 20th century life and has influenced great composers like Aaron Copland and Leonard Bernstein. And the new technology of computers and electronic instruments has had a major effect on the ways music is composed, performed and recorded.

- Claude Debussy *(1862–1918), Prelude to the Afternoon of a Faun*
- Maurice Ravel *(1875–1937), Bolero*
- Igor Stravinsky *(1882–1971), Rite of Spring*
- Sergei Prokofiev *(1891–1952), Classical Symphony, Peter and the Wolf*
- George Gershwin *(1898–1937), Rhapsody in Blue*
- Aaron Copland *(1900–1990), Appalachian Spring*
  - Leonard Bernstein *(1918–1990), West Side Story*

1900   **1925**   **1950**   **1975**   **2000**

ART & LITERATURE

- Robert Frost, author *(Stopping by Woods on a Snowy Evening)*
- Pablo Picasso, artist *(Three Musicians)*
- J.R.R. Tolkien, author *(The Lord of the Rings)*
- F. Scott Fitzgerald, author *(The Great Gatsby)*
- Andy Warhol, artist *(Pop art)*
- Salvador Dali, artist *(Soft Watches)*
- Norman Mailer, author *(The Executioner's Song)*
- John Steinbeck, author *(The Grapes of Wrath)*
- Ernest Hemingway, author *(For Whom the Bell Tolls)*
- Andrew Wyeth, artist *(Christina's World)*
- George Orwell, author *(1984)*

1900   **1925**   **1950**   **1975**   **2000**

WORLD EVENTS

- First airplane flight *(1903)*
- Television invented *(1927)*
- Berlin Wall built *(1961)*
- Destruction of Berlin Wall *(1989)*
- World War I *(1914–1918)*
- World War II *(1939–1945)*
- John F. Kennedy assassinated *(1963)*
- First radio program *(1920)*
- Civil rights march in Alabama *(1965)*
- First satellite launched *(1957)*
- Man walks on the moon *(1969)*
- Vietnam War ends *(1975)*
- Personal computers *(1975)*

Reproducible

Activity

NAME _____

DATE _____

1. The Middle Ages were also known as:
   A. the Twentieth Century
   B. the Medieval Period
   C. the Romantic Era

2. Gregorian chants were organized by:
   A. Pope Gregory
   B. Pope John
   C. Pope Paul

3. Church music was written down using neumes, which were notes shaped like:
   A. triangles
   B. circles
   C. squares

4. The church which had the most powerful influence in European life was:
   A. Roman Catholic
   B. Baptist
   C. Presbyterian

5. A form of music in which the harmony parts are independent melodies sung with the main tune is called:
   A. polyester
   B. polyphony
   C. polygraph

6. A famous book written during the Middle Ages is:
   A. Canterbury Tales
   B. Alice in Wonderland
   C. Little Women

7. Name three world events that happened during this time period:

8. Write a paragraph about what you think life would have been like in the Middle Ages.

Reproducible

HISTORY WORKSHEET • QUIZ
(The Renaissance)

NAME _____

DATE _____

1. The Renaissance lasted from:
   A. 1900–1925
   B. 1450–1600
   C. 1890–1900

2. The word "Renaissance" means:
   A. recycle
   B. return
   C. rebirth

3. Non-religious music is called:
   A. secular
   B. sacred
   C. symphony

4. Simple melodies in even rhythms like the hymns we still hear today are called:
   A. chants
   B. chorales
   C. operas

5. An important Renaissance composer was:
   A. Franz Schubert
   B. Martin Luther
   C. Thomas Tallis

6. An important invention that brought music to the homes of the middle class was:
   A. the printing press
   B. MTV
   C. the radio

7. A famous painting by Leonardo da Vinci is:
   A. Lisa Marie
   B. Mona Lisa
   C. Ramona Lee

8. Name three world events which occurred during the Renaissance:

Activity

NAME _____

DATE _____

1. The Baroque Era lasted from:
   A. 1400–1500
   B. 1900–1950
   C. 1600–1750

2. The most popular keyboard instrument was the:
   A. harpsichord
   B. synthesizer
   C. grand piano

3. Making up music using the composer's chords and bass line was called:
   A. improvising
   B. conducting
   C. arranging

4. Quick nearby tones added to decorate melodies were called:
   A. grace notes
   B. eighth notes
   C. instant notes

5. A famous violin maker in Italy was:
   A. Rubens
   B. Stradivarius
   C. Cervantes

6. A famous artist during the Baroque Era was:
   A. Defoe
   B. Rembrandt
   C. Swift

7. Match the following music with the name of the composer:
   ___Trumpet Tune   A. J.S. Bach
   ___The Messiah   B. Antonio Vivaldi
   ___The Four Seasons   C. Henry Purcell
   ___Peasant's Cantata   D. G.F. Handel

8. Name three world events that occurred during the Baroque Era:

Reproducible

HISTORY WORKSHEET • QUIZ
(The Classical Era)

Activity

NAME _____

DATE _____

1. The Classical Era lasted from:
   A. 1750–1820
   B. 1500–1600
   C. 1850–1900

2. Composers were employed to entertain:
   A. wealthy nobles and aristocrats
   B. farmers and migrant workers
   C. priests and church members

3. The instrument that replaced the harpsichord was the:
   A. trumpet
   B. viola
   C. piano

4. The favorite form of chamber music was the:
   A. string trio
   B. string quartet
   C. string quintet

5. A work for orchestra with four contrasting parts or movements is the:
   A. concerto
   B. sonata
   C. symphony

6. A mechanical device that helps musicians count was invented called the:
   A. time signature
   B. metronome
   C. rhythm

7. Name two composers of the Classical Era:

8. A famous artist in the Classical Era was:
   A. Goya
   B. Wordsworth
   C. Napoleon

9. Match the following books with the name of the author:
   ___Candide   A. Samuel Johnson
   ___Faust   B. Jane Austen
   ___Dictionary   C. Voltaire
   ___Pride and Prejudice   D. Goethe

Reproducible

147

HISTORY WORKSHEET • QUIZ
(The Romantic Era)

Activity

NAME _____

DATE _____

1. The Romantic Era lasted from:
   A. 1820–1900
   B. 1520–1600
   C. 1620–1700

2. The last compositions of this composer during the Classical Era were the first of the Romantic Era:
   A. Mozart
   B. Haydn
   C. Beethoven

3. An important trend in this era was:
   A. Imperialism
   B. Nationalism
   C. Socialism

4. Romantic music was usually very:
   A. dramatic
   B. grammatic
   C. problematic

5. Match the following music with the name of the composer:
   ___New World Symphony
   ___William Tell Overture
   ___Pomp and Circumstance
   ___The Nutcracker
   ___Barcarolle

   A. Gioacchino Rossini
   B. P.I. Tchaikovsky
   C. Jacques Offenbach
   D. Antonin Dvořák
   E. Edward Elgar

6. "Tom Sawyer" and "Huckleberry Finn" were both written by:
   A. Mark Twain
   B. Louise May Alcott
   C. Charles Dickens

7. "The Sunflowers" was a painting by:
   A. Claude Monet
   B. Pierre Renoir
   C. Vincent van Gogh

8. Name one thing that was invented during the era that still exists today. Then describe how this invention has affected our lives.

Reproducible

HISTORY WORKSHEET • QUIZ
(The 20th Century)

Activity

NAME _____

DATE _____

1. 20th century music was written during the:
   A. 1900s
   B. 1600s
   C. 1800s

2. Impressionistic music that seemed more vague and blurred than the Romantic Era was written by:
   A. Ravel and Debussy
   B. Bach and Beethoven
   C. Schoenberg and Stravinsky

3. Neo-classical music returned to the principles of balance and form that prevailed during the:
   A. Baroque Era
   B. Romantic Era
   C. Classical Era

4. Twelve-tone music was written so that it used:
   A. 12 different key signatures
   B. 12 tones of the chromatic scale
   C. 12 different rhythms

5. The way music was composed, performed, and recorded was greatly influenced by:
   A. technique
   B. technicality
   C. technology

6. Match the following music with the name of the composer:
   __Rhapsody in Blue
   __West Side Story
   __Bolero
   __Peter And The Wolf
   __Appalachian Spring

   A. Maurice Ravel
   B. Sergei Prokofiev
   C. Aaron Copland
   D. George Gershwin
   E. Leonard Bernstein

7. Match the following books with the name of the author:
   __The Great Gatsby
   __The Grapes of Wrath
   __For Whom The Bell Tolls

   A. Ernest Hemingway
   B. F. Scott Fitzgerald
   C. John Steinbach

8. Name two famous artists of the 20th century:

9. Name three world events that occurred during the 20th century. Then pick one and write a paragraph on how it has influenced your life today.

Reproducible

149

ANSWER KEY FOR HISTORY WORKSHEETS

MIDDLE AGES

1. B
2. A
3. C
4. A
5. B
6. A
7. Any of the following:
   Fall of Roman Empire
   Muhammad, prophet of Islam faith
   Hindu-Arabic numbers developed
   Gunpowder, compass, paper invented (China)
   Mayan civilization
   Charlemagne, Holy Roman Emperor
   First Crusade begins
   The Black Death (bubonic plague)
   Rise of European universities
   The Magna Charta
   Genghis Kahn rules Asia
   Marco Polo travels to China
   Incan and Aztec civilizations

THE RENAISSANCE

1. B
2. C
3. A
4. B
5. C
6. A
7. B
8. Any of the following:
   Gutenberg invents printing press
   Martin Luther ignites Protestant Reformation
   Columbus travels to America
   Magellan circles globe
   Copernicus begins modern astronomy
   First European contact with Japan

THE BAROQUE ERA

1. C
2. A
3. A
4. A
5. B
6. B
7. C, D, B, A
8. Any of the following:
   Galileo identifies gravity
   First English colony in America
   Quebec founded by Champlain
   First slaves to America
   Salem witchcraft trials
   Louis XIV builds Versailles Palace
   Isaac Newton formulates principals of physics and math

THE CLASSICAL ERA

1. A
2. A
3. C
4. B
5. C
6. B
7. Haydn, Mozart, Beethoven, or any others not listed in the book.
8. A
9. C, D, A, B

THE ROMANTIC ERA

1. A
2. C
3. B
4. A
5. D, A, E, B, C
6. A
7. C
8. Railroad, photography, telephone, phonograph, light bulb or movie projector

THE 20TH CENTURY

1. A
2. A
3. C
4. B
5. C
6. D, E, A, B, C
7. B, C, A
8. Picasso, Dali, Wyeth or Warhol
9. Any of the following:
   First airplane flight, Television invented
   Berlin Wall built
   Destruction of Berlin Wall World War I
   World War II,
   John F. Kennedy assassinated
   First radio program,
   Civil rights march in Alabama
   First satellite launched
   Man walks on the moon
   Vietnam War ends
   Personal computers

150